WITHDRAWN BY THE
UNIVERSITY OF MICHIGAN

SWING VOTERS
Understanding Late-Deciders
in Late-Modernity

CRITICAL BODIES
Joseph J. Pilotta, series editor

The Body in Human Inquiry:
  Interdisciplinary Explorations of Embodiment
    Vicente Berdayes, Luigi Esposito and John W. Murphy (eds.)

Swing Voting: Understanding Late-Deciders in Late-Modernity
    Philip D. Dalton

Educating For Participatory Democracy: Paradoxes in Globalizing Logics
    Roy O. Elveton

Knowledge and the Production of Non-knowledge:
  An Exploration of Alien Mythology in Post-War America
    Mark Featherstone

The New Age Ethic and the Spirit of Postmodernity
    Carmen Kuhling

Abjection and Its Correction in Ethnographic Studies
    Jill Adair McCaughan

Plato's Cave: Revised Edition
  Television and its Discontents
    John O'Neill

Why I [Still] Want My MTV
    Kevin Williams

forthcoming

Visceral Manifestation and the East Asian Communicative Body
    Jay Goulding

Phenomenology, Body Politics, and the Future of Communication Theory
    Hwa Yol Jung (ed.)

The Seductive Aesthetics of Post-Colonialism
    Rekha Menon

Body Works: Essays on Modernity and Morality
    John O'Neill

Tissues of Carnality
    Joseph Pilotta and Aligis Mickunas

SWING VOTERS
Understanding Late-Deciders in Late-Modernity

Philip D. Dalton
Stetson University

HAMPTON PRESS, INC.
CRESSKILL, NEW JERSEY

Copyright © 2006 by Hampton Press, Inc.

All rights reserved. No part of this publication may be reproduced, stored in a retrieval system, or transmitted in any form or by any means, electronic, mechanical, photocopying, microfilming, recording, or otherwise, without permission of the publisher.

Printed in the United States of America

Library of Congress Cataloging-in-Publication Data

Dalton, Philip D.
    Swing voters: understanding late-deciders in late-modernity / Philip D. Dalton
       p. cm. -- (The Hampton Press communication series. Critical bodies)
    Includes bibliographic references and index.
    ISBN 1-57273-654-2 -- ISBN 1-57273-655-0
1. Voting--United States. I. Title. II. Series

JK1967.D35 2005
324.973--dc22

                                                   2005055135

Hampton Press, Inc.
23 Broadway
Cresskill, NJ 07626

I am indebted to Oklahoma's taxpayers. Their tax dollars have produced one of the world's finest research institutions—the University of Oklahoma. Far more valuable than the sum of its costs, it is an institution for which the state's residents must be proud. I am truly honored to have studied there.

CONTENTS

FOREWORD	ix
Eric Mark Kramer	
INTRODUCTION	1
CHAPTER 1 – UNDERSTANDING SWING VOTERS	7
What Is the Swing Voter Phenomenon?	7
The Importance of Studying Swing Voters	15
Studying Swing Voters	18
Swing Voters as Audience	20
Political Communication Environment	24
CHAPTER 2 – DISCUSSION OF METHOD	29
Limitations of Natural Science Methodology	34
Methodology	37
Method of Analysis	45
Validity	47
CHAPTER 3 – INTERVIEWING SWING VOTERS	51
Overview of Analysis – Modern Voting	51

CHAPTER 4 – A HERMENEUTIC OF MODERN VOTING — 93
Characteristics and Origins of Modern Swing Voting — 93
Dimensional Accrual/Dissociation Theory — 95
Tracing the Origins of the Modern Swing Voter Attitude — 100
Modern Time and Eternal Truths — 105
Institutionalization of Modern Voting Participation — 108

CHAPTER 5 – PRIMACY OF THE PRIVATE SPHERE — 113
The Devolution of the Public Sphere — 113
Keeping it Real — 115
Political Communication Consumption — 125
Time Poverty — 131

CHAPTER 6 – ALTERITY AS NECESSITY — 135
Contemporary Self-Understanding — 136
The Value of Alterity — 139
Re-examining Contemporary Ontology Vis-á-Vis Civics — 142
What Are We To Do? — 150

APPENDIX A — 153

APPENDIX B — 155
Bush Spot: "No Changes/No Reductions" — 155
Gore spot: "College" — 156

References — 159
Author Index — 167
Subject Index — 171

FOREWORD

In this book Philip Dalton presents some of the first academically generated empirical data available on swing voter behavior, motives, and attitudes. He also presents the most extensive effort to date devoted to defining and identifying who the "swing voter" is. More importantly, he attempts to understand how swing voters come to finally make their voting choices. To this end, this book is not simply a recitation of data but rather Dalton has gone to great lengths to offer explanations of the data. Thus, this book suggests a new and very sophisticated theoretical framework for understanding voter decision making.

It is somewhat astonishing to realize that very little scholarly research has been done into the process swing voters follow in their efforts to come to voting decisions. This is especially the case when one considers that many elections in the United States are won by narrow margins, and that those margins that exist between the core of party loyalists is comprised largely of voters who make up their minds very late in the campaign process. Dalton demonstrates that the process by which swing voters come to decisions is quite different from the way party loyalists make their voting choices. Indeed, one could argue that the more intense party loyalists make no voting decisions at all but instead selectively perceive and argue for candidates and issues along partisan lines. It is the case that political campaign managers are well aware of this fact, and this is why so much money is used to produce messages targeting the coveted swing voter. Thus, it is understandable why, after quickly reassuring and activating the party base, most campaigns expend the bulk of their resources attempting to woo the indecisive swing voter. The party loyalist can be taken for granted.

The fact that swing voting is "the battleground" for many elections begs for this research. And this marginal area in the electorate is growing. Claims to be "centrist" and to "move to the center" are commonly enunciated as important campaign strategy. The center is coming to be a synonym for rational and reasonable, the "golden mean" of political persuasion. The center is, by definition, not extreme. Slogans such as "compassionate conservatism" and "fiscally conservative liberal" demarcate this discursive space. Ironically "the center," is seen as the *marginal* realm of decision making, being as it is outside party control.

Dalton argues that the center is the most rational and diligently meticulous sector of the electorate. It is where balance tends to maintain because ideological arrogance is humbled. Swing voters are the ones who seek information most tenaciously, sometimes believing even as they enter the voting booth that they still do not know enough to warrant such an important decision.

In the following volume, Dalton presents evidence gathered through careful interviewing that argues that swing voters are not indifferent, apolitical, cynical, or lazy voters. Instead, his data demonstrates that swing voters embody the ideal of civic responsibility as they hold off making decisions until late in elections, waiting to gather as much information as possible so as to not rush into rash choices. They prove to be very conscientious and rational decision makers. Due to their independent mindedness, they prove to not be easily or quickly convinced. Thus, the declining trend in party activism may signal that democracy in the United States is healthy at least with regard to a rising tide of independent thinking among the electorate. The true challenge is to protect the system from grossly unequal power distribution among special interests, mediated by party machines. Such an unequal playing field can have the deleterious effect of at least creating the impression that expending effort on making voting decisions is negated by powerful interests working to protect or even strengthen their own status within the system. The danger here, the definition of corruption, is the sense that individual votes "don't matter." Swing voters embody the faith that their votes do matter.

In the face of declining interests in party participation per se, the major parties have reacted with expected defensive postures and efforts at maintaining their organizational power and influence over the democratic process. Dalton's research indicates that the established parties have good reason to be concerned. More and more Americans are claiming to be "independents." Instead of seeing politics as a team sport, they are insisting that each candidate convince them, as individuals, why he or she deserves their vote. In the face of great voter apathy, Dalton is exploring the very marginal space where elections are increasingly fought and decided, where voters work hardest to make good decisions.

This book is essential reading for anyone interested in the political process in the United States and indeed, it has important implications for democracies everywhere. It points the way forward for future research into an exceptionally important area of political communication.

Eric Mark Kramer
Professor of Communication
The University of Oklahoma

ACKNOWLEDGMENTS

No different than most books, my work benefited from the contributions of the many who helped along the way. The route that took me to the conclusions found in this book was indirect and marked by numerous teachers. Most notable amoung these was Dr. Eric Kramer who encouraged me throughout this project and mentored me in my philosophy. For him I reserve a special thanks. In addition to my teachers, I've encountered individuals who've taken a speciial interest in my arguments. One such person, Sheridan Phillips, both edited this book and made theoretical suggestions; for this I am indebted. I would also like to thank the people who submitted to my interviews. While some appeared pleased to contribute, many, I fear, perceived themselves as badgered by an anxious graduate student ostensibly desparate for qualified and willing subjects. Finally, I would like to thank Stetson University for the resources they contributed to my writing effort.

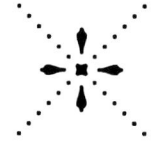

INTRODUCTION

This project was originally conceived as an attempt to better understand semiotically how swing voters assign meaning to presidential political advertisements. The scope of the project evolved, however, as it became evident that insight into much broader questions emerged from the interviews I conducted following the 2000 presidential election. Consequently, the reader will notice almost no emphasis on the political advertisements utilized to stimulate discussion with voters. Instead, underscored in this book is the general horizon of the swing voter. The word *horizon* is used in the hermeneutic sense of the word; "the horizon," according to Gadamer (1960/2000), "is the range of vision that includes everything that can be seen from a particular vantage point. . . . Since Nietzsche and Husserl, the word has been used in philosophy to characterize the way in which thought is tied to its finite determinacy and the way one's range of vision is gradually expanded" (p. 302). This is what the reader finds in this book, an explanation of the swing voter's horizon, characterized by modern ontological presuppositions, including a belief in the existence of an apprehendable or approximable totalized truth. To access such a truth, the voter models the scientist by squelching his/her passions in order to become a more pure observer. This is a mechanism that enables the management of the deluge of contextless and meaningless information encountered daily. So, this book can be characterized as a hermeneutic investigation of swing voters' horizons, helping to explain *how* and *why* they think or behave the ways they do with respect to politics.

Most of the writing I've encountered treats the swing-voting phenomenon as a side note while emphasizing almost exclusively the role of the partisan or the disaffected voter. Voters' behaviors often seem explained as the outcome of events and arguments unique to the particular election in question; they are the product of description and analysis of events suspected to have contributed to the outcome. Some analyze the advertisements, strategy, or rhetoric. Others study the economy, campaign funding, and party cohesion. Many readers are interested in why George W. Bush "won" or why Al Gore "lost" in 2000; antecedent factors, such as economic performance, job creation, foreign policy, gaffes, style, rhetoric, and/or charisma are relatively easy to marshal when theorizing or speculating about election outcomes *after* an election. The extent to which the types of questions asked and the methods employed to answer them limit our ability to understand the swing voter phenomenon as a cultural one is discussed in Chapter 1 and Chapter 2.

Some readers may observe similarities between the conclusions found in this book and those in Anthony Down's (1957) *An Economic Theory of Democracy*. These conclusions don't contrast much with the findings of V.O. Key (1966), Samuel Popkin (1991), or Martin Wattenberg (1991), either. Specifically, readers of these volumes have encountered the contention that swing voters are *not* necessarily lazy or uneducated, but are instead conscientious, concerned, and motivated, albeit with relatively less time with which to engage the system politically. This position is counterintuitive to some because of the general attitude that those who don't actively participate in politics are simply undermotivated couch potatoes or disenchanted dropouts. As I discuss the conclusions in this book with my students and friends, they typically react in one of three ways. The seemingly disenchanted students continue to seem disenchanted. The indignant reactions of very partisan students are perceived by me to be a product of attitudes valuing partisan preference and partisanship over any other democratic participatory modality. The most interesting reaction, however, is that evinced by those who are themselves swing voters (those disenchanted with parties and/or candidates though not politics). Their eyes light up and they smile. Something clicks with them as I describe the swing voter as conceived and described here. They smile and shake their heads in agreement in a way that connotes, "Finally, someone understands what *I'm* doing." The explanation of the phenomenon proffered in this book goes beyond the limited claim that swing voters reason and are rational about politics; it situates itself within the discussion and contributes something new by studying this group of voters *specifically* and submitting an account explaining *why* these voters think about politics and behave politically the ways they do.

Those interviewed in this project evidenced two types of swing voter. There were extrapartisan swingers and objective swingers. While this study focuses almost exclusively on the objective swing voters, extra-partisan swing voters warrant reckoning. Partisan swing voters, included among Ross Perot and Ralph Nader supporters, are those who "betray" their respective parties largely because they believe the parties have failed them. These are quasiphilosophical voters—meaning they support a creed, ideal, or policy, that informs their candidate selection. Republicans supporting Perot in 1992 betrayed George H. W. Bush largely because of Perot's strong support for balanced-budget measures, whereas Democrats supporting Nader in 2000 were alarmed by the state of the environment and the more general perception that the Democratic Party had abandoned its more humanistic principles in pursuit of centrist palatability. These voters were more ideological than many steadfast partisans and seem to be remarkably different from the objective swing voters discussed in this book

Perhaps the most significant limitation to this study is a result of the methodology, which involved interviewing late-deciding voters. Among all of the most obvious limitations interview-based research faces, social-desirability bias features prominently particularly in this project considering its political subject matter; recruiting involved the systematic pursuit of the politically reticent to discuss politics on videotape with a stranger. Considering the circumstances, it is unlikely that the reactions elicited during these interviews would not be influenced by the participants' perception that certain answers are correct or preferred by the interviewer. This criticism ignores, however, two important things. First, if subjects are simply telling me what they feel I want to hear, at the very least they are revealing what they believe is the culturally accepted approach to voting. This revelation, in and of itself, is of value as these perceptions undoubtedly shape the voters' own attitudes about voting. Suspicion of social-desirability bias's influence might seem more valid if the voters involved in the interviews didn't continually criticize *their own* approach to politics relative to what they expressed was *ideal* participation. It is quite clear that they weren't trying to impress me. Second, I contend that there *is* reason to believe that what swing voters maintain is a socially desirable mode of participation is significantly different from partisans' perceptions. In other words, while the responses of participants may seem too good to be true, in light of the presumed attitudes that many readers are presumed to have of swing voters, the ideas about political participation emergent from discussions with these voters are neither obvious nor intuitive. Instead, because they are not in keeping with our most celebrated political traditions, which value exhibitions of public concern and deliberative involvement, swing voter comments are seemingly inexplicable; how are we to account for them?

Our inability to apprehend swing voters' attitudes and motivations may be the result of the limited models we have for understanding the variety of attitudes that govern behavior in our political system. It seems that dialectical forces are credited with shaping different approaches to voting—one force tending toward organization and the other toward chaos. Most discourse relative to politics organizes information according to this framework; on one hand political parties are organized ideally around a "philosophy" or (to be more accurate) a platform, while on the other hand, there are those who have chosen to opt out of the system. Relying on this spectrum, observers are led to perceive voters as either more or less partisan. In terms of the current discussion, the most obvious fault with this linear framework is that it fails to make sense of those voters who decide late. If one is partisan and ostensibly politically engaged, s/he should know for whom s/he will vote. Likewise, one should predict that those who don't vote are less engaged and politically knowledgeable. This logic should place swing voters somewhere between the extremes: relatively less knowledgeable and engaged. This inadequately explicates why participants in this study were as conscientious about their decisions as they proved to be. The reasoning buttressing this spectrum is circular; as long as the measure of valuable engagement is partisan participation, those less partisan will always appear to be relatively less engaged. If voter engagement, however, is redefined according to some measure or expression of *concern* for election outcomes, it is likely that devoted partisans and swing voters would be characterized similarly. This disrupts the logic of a dialectical understanding of these phenomena—perhaps it adds another dimension.

One particular value articulated by the swing voters in this project helps explain swing voters in a way that the dialectical perspective failed to do; these voters expressed a desire to be as objective (fair and distanced) and as informed as possible. According to the participants involved in this project, voters with predispositions were going about decision making fundamentally incorrectly. According to the swing voter's vantage point, prejudging candidates according to a preexisting value structure results in a tainted or less-exact decision. The value of objectivity precludes partisan involvement as well as issue-oriented voting, because these practices are evidence of bias and/or closed-mindedness. How can this be? If the primary political socializing institutions are the political parties, then the origins of the swing-voter horizon require explanation. After all, this way of constituting politics couldn't just spring from the ether.

Chapters 4 and 5 offer the reader an explanation for much of this. I argue that the swing voter is part of something larger—it is an individualistic trend that began with the Renaissance and is now finding a fuller but deficient expression in our culture. The value of the ego has outranked community obligation. Society slackened its hold upon the individual for its ultimate benefit or preservation; modern cities and states became much too large and diverse to compel behavior consistent with community mores, taboos, and codes, becoming more tolerant as a result. Order and justice were maintained by striking a delicate balance between authoritative goodwill (freedom) and individual community obligation. Today however, this balance has shifted; society is believed to function to preserve and protect liberty—not the other way around. Individual interests have become paramount. Jean Gebser (1949/1985), Lewis Mumford (1951), Jules Henry (1965), Vance Packard (1974), and Robert Putnam (2000) and many others have contributed to our understanding of the sociological phenomenon characterized by community disengagement and the pursuit of individual interests—liberty. This means people don't engage their communities, don't have opinions, have no context, no ground.

When community is lost, political parties make less sense. The modern solution is objectivity or politics at a distance. The voter observes and decides, though never involves: s/he never stirs the pot. Still, no alarms are going off. The impression of an animated and healthy public sphere is projected to us by our television sets. We sit at home quickly clicking past C-Span to occasionally catch a moment of Bill O'Reilly or Sean Hannity engaging someone in a visceral exchange with a caller or guest. Mass media products give us the impression the public sphere is alive and well, but beyond the veil there is little reason today to believe this is actually true.

One could throw his/her hands in the air and retreat more completely behind the walls of his/her home or privacy fence, after all, it seems to be what everyone else is doing. This, however, doesn't lead us anywhere better: an unsatisfactory proposition for a society so concerned with progress. Taken to its ultimate end, individualism becomes chaos—communication becomes cacophony. Chapter 6 explores the ontological presuppositions of modernity and individualism, offering a critique condemning our blind observance to rationality's demands. Criticism of modernity has become a trite practice in academia, and I don't wish for these arguments to be lumped with the rest. I believe that my point is more nuanced, traversing carefully the minefields between modernity and postmodernity. Influenced by the phenomenological works of Gebser, Maurice Merleau-Ponty, and Emmanuel Levinas, I maintain that the ego has fallen victim to the totalizing tendencies of modernity; the self pursues "full-expression" or "actualization" at the expense of all else. The result is alienation: our neighbors become strangers and our children acquaintances. Unique is that I don't promote a return to a mythic political utopia based on self-denial and naiveté. Instead, I argue that an enlightened awareness of an integral understanding of human waring is necessary to appreciate the mythic and magic fulfillment that comes from belonging *to* and participating *with* a community. The Other calls us forth to watch, serve, and celebrate his/her alterity. The imperative of the Other is a preunderstanding upset by modernity which pulls us back by prioritizing self above all else. It is suggested that modernity not be rejected but tempered by an awareness about what modernity *means* in light of the other modes of waring and our obligations to those other than ourselves.

1

UNDERSTANDING SWING VOTERS

> In contemporary elections it is common for political consultants to divide voters into advertising segments based on public opinion polls and focus groups: the committed (those who are for you), the hopeless (those who are against you and about whom little can be done), and the undecided (those who could vote either way). The last group, of course, is the central target of campaign tactics.
>
> Darrell M. West

WHAT IS THE SWING VOTER PHENOMENON?

What is a swing voter? The question is an important one due to the group's size and potential power. Because of their ability to decide any given election, this is a question that consumes the time of the professional campaign practitioners who devote themselves to the operation of political campaigns. Campaign practitioners play a significant role in the operation of our democratic system though their success is measured by their ability to garner attention for someone else: the candidate. For instance, the average voter is unlikely able to identify Donna Brazil as Al Gore's presidential campaign manager in 2000 or Karl Rove as George W. Bush's campaign administrator. Despite their relatively low profiles, campaign practitioners' burdens are enormous. They are charged with the responsibility of pursuing the hearts and minds of potential voters, a task that devours vast sums of money (e.g., Devlin, 1989; Devlin, 1993; Devlin, 1997; Devlin, 2001). Devlin (2001) states that President Bush broke all records in campaign advertisement expenses, spending $134 million on the 2000 general election; $28 million more than Al Gore. Jefrey Pollock, president of Global Strategy Group and lecturer at Columbia University, identifies the need to focus attention on swing voters as the 5th Commandment of Campaigning (Pollock, 2003).

> ... in order to win, you need actual voters. The floors are littered with "endorsed candidates" who end up losing to the ones who raise more money and persuade more swing voters. ... Find the swing voters, and target them with all of your campaign tools. (p. 10)

This advice would be helpful if it weren't so simplistic. A greater challenge is understanding what it means. Who are these voters?

While the term "swing voter" can be found in the discourse of campaign practitioners, it is difficult to find any formal definition. Wattenberg (1991) comes closest when he identifies and describes "floating voters." Wattenberg seems to be discussing the same group as Pollock (2003), in that he identifies voters whom campaigns covet most. Wattenberg explains that:

> ... such individuals have tuned out the parties but not necessarily the candidates and the issues. Indeed, they are often considered the most important group in American electoral politics. (p. 43)

The use of "floating voters" as a label for this population was a deliberate choice intended to avoid the sense of permanence connoted by "swing voters" who, once swung, are anchored.[1] In any case, in more general terms, these voters are politically nonhabitual, neither partisans nor nonvoters (Downs, 1957).

The differences between the labels "swing voter" and "floating voter" are significant and reflect the difficulty in understanding them. The floating voter floats. The entailments related to the metaphor of "floating" are important because something that floats may either move or stay relatively still. Once the floating object is grounded, it is no longer floating but anchored and static; a nonfloating voter becomes a partisan or a "drop-out," a nonparticipant.

---

[1] E-mail correspondence with Martin P. Wattenberg, 4/21/03.

A swinging voter, however, implies movement. Thus, a swing voter would move between parties, voting for the Democratic Party in one election, the Republican in another. Someone who "leans" Democratic wouldn't be a swing voter by definition. This plays out in survey research, which typically groups "leaners" among other partisans (Campbell, 2000).

These small and seemingly subtle semantic differences have proven to be important in conversations I have had regarding my research. For instance, people ask, "How do you know a swing voter has swung if you are interviewing them before the election?" Because subjects were interviewed *after* the 2000 election, problems related to this question were avoided; participants identified themselves as having chosen their candidate in the weekend prior to election day. Answering the same question is much more difficult for campaign practitioners who, to be successful, have the task of accurately anticipating voter trends and identifying the driving forces behind them. Holding fast to preconceived notions about the constitution of this group is unlikely to be helpful as key swing voting populations can change from election to election and from month to month.

This lack of definitional clarity contributes to the difficulty of developing a better understanding of this group. Very often "swing voter" is employed without reference to any specific parameters used to help define the group. Throughout academic literature, many words are used interchangeably with "swing voter" (e.g., Lazarsfeld, Berelson, & Gaudet, 1948; Key, 1966; Wattenberg, 1991). Nevertheless, a thorough analysis of campaign and voting literature helps explain what is typically implied by the phrase. There are three primary characteristics to this group. First, it is maintained here, though it is not universally accepted, that swing voters and other voters are similarly educated and interested in politics despite the former's late-decidedness. Second, swing voters can be either party-affiliated or self-identified independents; just because a voter is registered with a particular party does not indicate a strict allegiance to that party. Many states require a voter to register with a party just to participate in a primary, causing voters to claim a party affiliation when, in fact, they may have little or no proclivity toward either. Third, these voters are the undecided voters. Though these late-deciding voters are not the population of voters typically referred to when someone speaks of swing-voters, swing voters who have made up their mind are of little relevance to people managing campaigns. Instead, the swing voter group, at any given time during a campaign, includes any voter still capable of swinging. Although these characteristics are necessarily nebulous, they contribute to the definition and understanding of the active dynamic(s) of the phenomenon.

First Characteristic: Swing Voters as Engaged and Educated

Most contention centers on this first characteristic; the notion that swing voters and partisans are similarly interested in politics and similarly educated may seem counterintuitive to some. There exists a tendency in recent scholarship both to lament the growth of the politically-ignorant and to study the antecedents suspected to have contributed to their condition. From a democratic perspective, both ignorance and disengagement are inherently antideliberative, making these qualities potentially harmful both to the individual and the system. Although some studies may control for education while measuring political interest and participation, we shouldn't lose sight of Putnam's (2000) observation that today's U.S. citizen is as knowledgeable about politics as his/her grandparents. Still, the perception of the ignorant voter persists, contributing to the first of two seemingly different characterizations of the swinging-indecisive-voter phenomenon that have emerged in political scholarship. The first characterization maintains that swing voters are less engaged, less educated, and more ignorant about politics (Campbell, Converse, Miller, & Stokes, 1960). Packard (1957) documents the cynical attitudes held by political advertising researchers ("depth probers") and executives who characterized swing voters as less thoughtful, listless, and in one case, "snotty" (p. 183). Additionally, Downs (1957), Wattenberg (1991), and Popkin (1991) each maintain that some voters use shortcuts. To be fair, none of these authors condemns the apartisan reliance upon heuristics. As a matter of fact, some applaud the existence of such decision-making rules because they indicate a preference by some voters for reason over passion. Unavoidable, however, is the conclusion that good, proper, or thorough reasoning has been compromised by the use of such shortcuts.

In keeping with this characterization, Campbell, Converse, Miller, and Stokes (1960) have argued that the increasing number of individuals who vote independent of partisan affiliation is a potentially harmful development. They describe these voters as "conflicted," less educated, "less enthusiastic," possessing "poorly developed attitudes," and as "somewhat less involved in politics." Lazarsfeld, Berelson, and Gaudet (1948) consider these voters more "withdrawn" and "living within narrower horizons" (though still engaged and conflicted) (p. 70). More contemporary authors have reinforced these judgments: Berger (2000) argues, "political ads target the apolitical. Those that are disengaged sitting at home" (p. 69). Some of these characterizations are supported by research conducted by Lucas and Adams (1978) and Zaller (1998). Specifically, Zaller (1998) found that those more politically knowledgeable are more firmly anchored, less centrist, and more resilient to messages that oppose their predispositions. These characterizations stand to reason, but they don't necessarily support the belief held by many that the politically knowledgeable are exclusively partisan. Based upon the results of this project, I side with the notion that swing voters are generally engaged and conscientious political participants. Although the growth of partisan disaffection may be indicative of political disinterest, it may also indicate a reduction in partisan prejudice among the remaining population of voters.

Without *partisan* decision rules, how do apartisans vote? Iyengar and Petrocik (2000) explain that, for voting purposes, independent voters rely on assessments of candidate performance instead of partisan heuristics. Wattenberg (1991) makes this same point, explaining that voters increasingly engage in "performance based voting." Instead of relying on partisan bias to determine one's vote, the aforementioned authors maintain that voters are rationally assessing candidates' records and positions. Additionally, Key (1966) found no reason to believe that the group he termed "switchers" differed educationally from other types of voters:

> In short, the data make it appear sensible to regard the voter as a person who is concerned with what governments have done or not done and what they propose to do . . . (p. 41)

This position is consonant with Downs (1957) who generally maintains that all voters make rational decisions that benefit their self-interests. Moreover, Wattenberg (1991) adds that floating voters are increasingly likely to cite issue-based reasons for their votes. Iyengar and Petrocik (2000) add that independent voters base their votes on perceptions and evaluations of incumbent performance. Interestingly, Popkin (1991) argues that voter reasoning is rarely *characterized* by observers as reasonable because of the reduced amount of information and time available to the voter to help make well-reasoned decisions. Still, it seems their decisions are less influenced by partisan predispositions.

A less parsimonious understanding, favored here because of its explanatory power, maintains that swing voters fit both characterizations: their indecision is mistaken for indifference, disinterest, or disaffection. In conjunction with perception of limited efficacy, time demands, and other constraints, these voters are looking for solid ground upon which to justify their decisions. Swing voters put off their decision with the hopes that the revelation of new or additional information will ultimately make this choice more clear. This approach is supported by theory. Specifically, Gebser (1949/1985) and Kramer (1997) give good reason to believe that swing voters' lack of decisiveness, traditional participation, and emotional involvement is not necessarily an indication of a lack of interest. These theoretical contributions contribute to the explications in future chapters, showing that the emotional distance swing voters exhibit is evidence of a unique manner of involvement. Their theories maintain that one characteristic of rational consciousness is a decrease in emotional involvement accompanied by increased dependence upon reason. This is termed "distanciation." Gebser's (1949/1985) and Kramer's (1997) ideas help reconcile what appear to be two contradictory characterizations. Their ideas are essential to understanding the findings presented in this book, and they will be developed at length later.

Second Characteristic: Swing Voters as Party-Affiliated or Independent

Swing voters can be either affiliated with a major party or registered independents. Note that I'm being careful here to distinguish between extrapartisan voters and late-deciding swing voters. Extrapartisans are those voters whose candidate selection wavers due to their ideology, philosophy, or issue preferences that shape their choices. For instance, a Republican may have chosen to support Texas businessperson Ross Perot because of Perot's support for a balanced budget. This voter refuses to compromise his/her beliefs for the sake of party solidarity. Though such voters may wait until the last minute to choose between the major party and a third party candidate, I maintain that they (extrapartisans) are not those intended when individuals reference swing voters. In contrast to extrapartisans are voters similar to Key's (1966) switcher (voters capable of switching their votes from candidates of one party to candidates of another between elections). According to Key, "switching parties" means voting for candidates of different parties and not necessarily changing one's party identification. These voters can be either self-professed partisans *or* independents. He argues that these people do not differ educationally from partisans and are just as interested in politics as other voters. The most significant difference between swing voters (switchers) and early deciding partisan voters is that swing voters tend to have a greater likelihood of switching parties over the long-run.

Similar to Key's ideas are Wattenberg's (1991) observations pertaining to floating voters he identifies as "the most important group in American electoral politics" (p. 43). These voters are targeted by campaigns *exactly* because of their propensity to change allegiances. His analysis of National Election Studies (NES) data reveals that floating voters make more neutral or balanced comments about politicians and parties regardless of their professed independence or party preference, suggesting that they are not assessing candidates from a partisan vantage point. They seem less likely to rely on partisan affiliations for help with decision making; they depend on both issues and perceptions of candidate performance.

Although the observation that swing voters possess the capacity to swing between candidates of different parties may seem rather obvious, it is important to note that this alone defines the group and not their "independence" from party identification. Independent voters are technically defined as those who identify themselves as such when they register with their state to vote. Regardless of their official identification on state election rosters, independent voters may be anything but independent from partisan sympathy. Wattenberg (1991) maintains that while many independents tend to be more partisan than they are given credit for, party members are decreasingly willing to identify themselves as such.[1] The trouble with the meaning of the term *swing voter* stems from writers who use terms like *independent, nonpartisan,* and *ticketsplitters* (e.g., Ansolabehere & Iyengar, 1996; Joslyn, 1984) interchangeably without devoting much effort to clarifying what constitutes these groups. Although independents may compose part of the swing vote in a given election, so may registered partisans. Iyengar and Petrocik's (2000) observations undermine the notion that swing voters are made up solely of independents. Their work maintains that partisans and registered independents vote according to "basic rules" (p. 119). Specifically, they claim that it is generally true that partisans vote for their parties' slated candidate whereas independent votes are based upon their assessments of incumbent performance. The data that support this claim, however, also reveal that a noticeable proportion of partisan voters fail to follow these general rules. This group of partisans, willing to vote on performance or rationales *other* than party loyalty, is important because their proportion is often larger than the difference between candidates leading up to an election, a difference that gives them the power to decide presidential elections (Fenwick, Wiseman, Becker, & Heiman, 1985).

Third Characteristic: Swing Voters as Late Deciders

So far this profile of a thoughtful, conscientious swing voter includes both late and early deciders. Yet, early deciders, having decided early, are no longer vacillating between candidates and as such are of little interest to the campaign practitioner. Having formulated their decisions, there is less reason to devote precious campaign resources to persuade them. For instance, a voter may assess a candidate's performance very early in a campaign and choose to re-elect him/her. Having developed his/her preference early, these voters are less likely to be persuaded, thus there would be no reason for the candidates' advertisements to pursue him/her (Kirkpatrick, 1972).

Implied in nearly all uses of swing voter and other related phrases are degrees of undecidedness. Targeting communication efforts at this key group has the potential to pay dividends, whereas advertising to voters faithful to the opponent's party would waste valuable campaign resources (Kirkpatrick, 1972). Lazarsfeld, Berelson, and Gaudet (1948) first attempted to explain who these voters are ("September-to-November voters" they termed them) and why they behave as they do. They explain that these voters experience "cross-pressures" defined as "the conflicts and inconsistencies among the factors which influence vote decision" (p. 53). These cross-pressures drive the voters in opposite directions.

---

[1] Longitudinal studies of NES data, Wattenberg (1991) observes, show a reduced willingness among voters to identify themselves as partisan though their behavior is consistent with that of partisans.

> . . . it is difficult for them to make up their minds simply because they had good reasons for voting for both candidates. Sometimes such reasons were so completely balanced that the decision had to be referred to a third factor for settlement. The doubt as to which was the better course—to vote Republican or to vote Democrat—combined with the process of self-argument caused the delay in the final vote decision for such people. (p. 130)

These observations have been echoed and developed by subsequent scholars.

Several behavioral and attitudinal characteristics of these conflicted late-deciders have been identified. In addition to the observation about conflict introduced by Lazarsfeld, Berelson, and Gaudet (1948), Kirkpatrick (1972) argues that some voters often delay their voting decision when they prefer one candidate but expect another to win (p. 399). He goes on to argue that cross-pressures contribute to election avoidance, withdrawal, and fluctuation. Campbell, Converse, Miller, and Stokes (1960) add that these voters also cast their votes with less enthusiasm. Lucas and Adams (1978) identify two characteristics of undecideds: they discuss politics less often with others and watch less network television news. To resolve the pressures these conflicted voters experience, Lazarsfeld, Berelson, and Gaudet (1948) explain that undecideds usually delay their decisions because of a lack of interest or until an event comes along that helps them resolve their conflict.

Hopefully, the reader develops from this discussion an appreciation for the difficulty inherent in operationally defining something as nebulous as the swing voter. Any voter can become a swing voter and any swing voter may stop swinging. A swing voter may leave the ranks and become a strict partisan. Traditional nonvoters can always choose to vote and swing an election. Likewise, voters with consistent voting histories may suddenly choose to abstain. Thus, consistent participation is not a prerequisite for being a swing voter. A voter may swing for one election and cease to swing thereafter. Conversely during a particular campaign, a swing voter may decide early, leaving her/him to swing no more until during a subsequent election, he or she swings once again. Campaigns are left to marshal their resources in pursuit of this amorphous and fickle entity; a group whose aggregate profile changes as the election draws near. Unfortunate for campaign practitioners is the knowledge that the individuals constituting this group can never be fully known until after the election. It is only after the election that one can begin to investigate who actually voted. Until that time, swing voters, such as soccer moms and Perot voters, are known as undecided voters (Jamieson, 2000).

THE IMPORTANCE OF STUDYING SWING VOTERS

Ron Faucheux (2003) editor-in-chief of *Campaigns and Elections* magazine, details just how pivotal swing voters are in presidential elections. He observes, "America is, in reality, a 30-30 nation: with about 30 percent of the electorate solidly Republican, 30 percent committed Democratic, 35 to 36 percent in the middle" (p. 7). These "middle" voters, he explains, do not support the parties and are characterized by their aversion to them.

> The fact that the middle bloc is larger than either party's base is the key to the future of American politics. This big chunk of voters is not enamored with either party. In fact, most of them are repelled by the whole idea of partisanship. . . . [I]f and when these middle-ground voters swing heavily to either side, as opposed to splitting nearly down the middle the way they've done in recent elections, they have the power to realign the entire political system. (p. 7)

Possessing this much power, it comes as little surprise that discourse of presidential candidates is tailored almost exclusively to the presumed interests and anxieties of swing voters. Brooks (2000) aptly explains that successful contemporary politicians are those capable of "reconciling" ideas between left and right. The capable politician, he explains, can "weave together different approaches. They triangulate. They reconcile. They know they have to appeal to diverse groups. They seek a Third Way beyond old categories of left and right" (p. 256). For example, according to *USA Today* President Bush uses his "compassionate conservative" theme to appeal to "swing voters" (Lawrence, April, 24, 2003, p. 8A). *Newsweek* explains that presidential campaign advisers devote themselves to identifying who occupies the swing population (Breslau, August, 28, 2000, p. 28). The article continues, stating that this group has manifested itself as "Reagan Democrats," "angry white males," and "soccer moms." Increasingly, the campaign practitioner's job is to find out who these people are with the hopes of learning how to most compellingly communicate with them. These concerns are not necessarily new. The Bush and Gore campaigns shared a great deal with past presidents, as even the 1948 presidential race between Truman and Dewey was influenced by a relatively large number of undecided voters. Even Roosevelt feared loosing the 1944 election because of the substantial number of late-deciders, estimated at 10 million voters (Barnouw, 1968).

While the channels of communication have evolved since 1944 from radio to television (and increasingly the Internet), the audience remains the same. Joslyn (1984) called this group of voters the "battleground of the electoral politics" (p. 59). That swing voters constitute the primary audience of campaign communication is significant because of their dulling effect on political deliberation. Political messages tailored to them are not as much "dumbed down" as they are "watered down" to help make political agendas more palatable. Politicians are more concerned with alienation than with persuasion. As is often the case when people try hard not to offend anyone, they are found to have little of interest to say; politicians are not immune to this phenomenon.

Although swing-voter impact on campaign discourse and policy proposals is a significant matter, so are the effects these voters have had on the political parties themselves. Party efforts to court the middle ground have contributed to, what Wattenberg (1991) terms "party disunity." Disillusionment with the party system is worth investigation because of the integral role of parties, either major or minor, in our contemporary democratic system. Patterson (1998) observes:

> Political parties give direction and strength to the people's votes. Through their numbers, citizens have the potential for great influence, but that potential cannot be realized unless they have the capacity to act together. Parties give them that capacity. (p. 342)

Patterson (1994) makes clear his belief that no other institution, as yet devised, functions as well to give voters a collective voice. Unfortunately, a lack of faith in the party system's willingness to provide support for the issues with which the voter identifies can ultimately result in a loss of support for these institutions. Whereas Campbell (2000) argues that the numbers don't show a reduction in partisanship, Wattenberg (1991) points out that what is disturbing is people's willingness to reject party identification when asked, even though they may qualify, by virtue of their voting history for example, as either a Democrat or Republican. Today's partisan is not what she/he used to be.

There is also concern about the nature of the discourse used to court centrist voters. The perception that late-deciding swing voters are less educated and less involved is likely to influence how one approaches the selection of messages and appeals. Packard (1957) explains that campaigns try to develop an "emotional pull" between voters and candidates (p. 183). Schwartz (1973) reinforces this point, and adds that this is done by "delivering" the voter to the candidate, as opposed to the other way around (p. 82). Essentially, this means that the campaign attempts to develop a situation wherein the voter draws a conclusion on his/her own because of salient attitudes and feelings fostered or "struck" by an advertisement. This is achieved by studying the voter in order to produce the advertisement that will best resonate with him/her. West (1993) states that this is achieved by pretesting advertisements, using focus groups, and extensive polling. This testing is likely to be done in a fashion similar to that described by Gitlin (1983), wherein respondents are recruited, subjected to video, and tested for responses. These responses are measured with buttons, dials, surveys, and even brain sensors (Tierney, 2004) from which quantitatively and qualitatively derived conclusions are drawn. In order for political advertisements to be effective, teams of pollsters, often headed by regulars on the talk-show pundit circuit like Dick Morris, Stan Greenberg, Paul Begala, and Frank Luntz, are hired to help determine who the swing voters are in a given election (Breslau, August 28, 2000). Professional techniques like these generate suspicion and cause communication scholars to study, describe, and/or criticize the non-rational nature of political advertisements (e.g., Packard, 1957; Drumwright, 1993; Caywood & Preston, 1989; Colford & Lafeyette, 1991; Richards & Caywood, 1991; Tinkham & Weaver-Larisay, 1994).

Finally, if those who suspect that swing voters are relatively less engaged are correct after all, then perhaps a more thorough understanding of the way they constitute politics will offer a glimpse into the psyche of those who are completely disaffected. Because of the value placed on political participation, abstainers concern many who study U.S. elections (e.g., Johnson, Hays, & Hays, 1998). Nearly half of eligible U.S. voters fail to participate (Miroff, Seidelman, & Swanstrom, 1999). Addressing this matter 40 years ago, Schattschneider (1960) wrote:

> In the past seven presidential elections the average difference in the vote cast for the winning candidates was about one-fifth as large as the total number of nonvoters. The unused political potential is sufficient to blow the United States off the face of the earth. (p. 97)

The problem is more disconcerting today. In the 2000 presidential election 66% of respondents between the ages of 18 and 29 reported that they did not vote, while 71% of respondents 65 or older stated that they voted. The *Washington Post* reports that "If current trends continue, the number of 65 and older who vote in midterm elections is likely to exceed that of young adults by a 4 to 1 ratio by 2022" (Goldstein & Morin, 2002, October 20, p. A01). As a result issues addressed by politicians increasingly reflect the needs and interests of older U.S. citizens. This results in a cycle of disengagement as younger voters fail to recognize the relationship between government and their own lives. Understanding why voters abstain is an important pursuit understood as an essential step in finding ways to inspire these voters to develop consistent voting habits. Because some read swing voter indecision as symptomatic of disengagement (Hart, 1999) it is maintained that this analysis of swing voters, though admittedly unique from disengaged voters, provides valuable insight into the attitudes, anxieties, and concerns with which contemporary voters cope.

Studying Swing Voters

Despite their centrality to campaigns, political communication research focusing on this group is rarely conducted. Because well-developed definitions were hard to come by much of the aforementioned literature was used to inform an operationalization unique to this study. For the purposes of this project swing voters were generally characterized as late-deciding voters—voters who were "swinging" between, or floating and uncommitted to, either candidate until the final days of the campaign. Because of the paucity of swing voter research, this project is an initial and exploratory attempt at understanding who swing voters are; it mainly attempts to explain how and why they constitute politics the ways that they do. Additionally, I speculate about the sociological meanings and implications of their attitudes. Fitting of such an exploratory project, the method employed is a fusion of ethnography and hermeneutics.

Ethnography requires the investigator to enter into the culture being studied (Geertz, 1973). The act of entering this culture presented a unique challenge to the project because, as I assumed prior to the project and feel justified in professing now, this group does not exhibit any obvious characteristics of "groupness." They do not gather anywhere in particular. They do not talk a certain way. Even when in one another's company it is unlikely that their swinging nature or partisan ambiguity is even a saliency, especially considering our culture's taboo against public talk of politics, religion, and personal finance. Though a person may enter into a new culture, and thus learn of or accrue new attitudes or cultural predispositions, they are not capable of losing or "unlearning" their prior culture. For instance, I don't walk around during my day conscious of myself as a Chicagoan, nevertheless, this facet of my history and the attitudes with which it imbues me are ever-present. My "Chicago-ness" does not go away just because I am not thinking about it at the moment. Swing voters, however, are unique in that, for them, there is no place to leave unless they leave the United States altogether for a new political system. Though on its face, this group does not fit the traditional conceptualization of a culture, it is still maintained that they constitute a cultural phenomenon fostered by the larger political milieu. This project was faced with the expected challenges inherent to ethnography, that of actually "entering" into a culture and gaining genuine access to its rules and attitudes. Finally, given the unique nature of this cultural group, I was careful not to presuppose that swing voters even constituted a cultural phenomenon without finding first evidence to support such a presumption. That they do constitute a cultural phenomenon is one of the more important findings elucidated throughout the book.

The hermeneutic analyses conducted in this project is primarily influenced by Hans-Georg Gadamer (1960/2000, 1977). The hermeneut attempts to "show the prephilosophical understanding of man in the world" which makes his/her interpretations of that world possible (Stewart & Mickunas, 1990, p. 145). In this respect, this project is closely related to Husserl's (Cartesian Mediations) notion of genetic phenomenology, a mode of cultural analysis that maintains that meaning is generated by preunderstandings shaped by accrued and sedimented cultural experiences. This study is conducted by fusing horizons; my horizon encountering and interpreting the horizons of the participants of this study. In so doing, the horizons of these individuals, and their prejudices, are explained. As is the case with hermeneutics, prejudices are not necessarily prejudgments made about others, like the decision to lock the car doors because of the perceived nature of the neighborhood through which one drives. Instead, Gadamer's notion of prejudices equip us to engage the world. Gadamer (1977) explains:

> It can be shown that the concept of prejudice did not originally have the meaning we have attached to it. Prejudices are not necessarily unjustified and erroneous, so that they inevitably distort the truth. In fact, the historicity of our existence entails that prejudices, in the literal sense of the word, constitute the initial directedness of our ability to experience. Prejudices are biases of our openness to the world. They are simply conditions whereby we experience something—whereby what we encounter says something to us. (p. 9)

Prejudice, according to Gadamer's use of the word, is necessary.

Certainly, Gadamer's (1977) notion of prejudice upsets the prejudices of many readers who presuppose that the world they perceive *is* the world that is positively and verifiably "out there" as they perceive it. Termed "correspondence theory," the latter prejudice presumes that our cognitive impressions relate precisely to the objects we encounter. According to Husserl (1954/1970), however, it is argued that individuals play an active role in synthesizing their world, but not in any conscious sort of way. Instead, we anticipate this world; it is pre-given. This act of synthesis is the process of "intending." How we intend our world constitutes our "natural attitude" (p. 145). The different attitudes possessed by people, or Gadamer's related "horizons," are what are subjected to analysis in this project.

Hermeneutics and its companion phenomenology are also inherently critical practices. Unlike the ethnographer, the hermeneut attempts to understand the origins of a culture's prejudices or preunderstandings and their implications. This is to be performed by studying the lifeworld (*lebenswelt*) as revealed in artifacts of a given culture. In this case, the discourse of participants is studied. Gadamer (1977) explains that a culture's traditions are embedded in its use of discourse:

> . . . human linguisticality [is] a limitless medium that carries everything within it—not only the "culture" that has been handed down to us through language, but absolutely everything . . . (p. 25)

Thus, the medium of language, and communication more generally, is analyzed. Intrinsic in the use of language is evidence of the attitudes the user possesses, though the hermeneut does not look to the language exclusively. These attitudes constitute unique facets of cultures developed to cope with or overcome cultural exigencies. The origins of these attitudes become sedimented, and over time simply become the world as given. A culture's attitudes function like a trajectory or inertia, seeming to propel individuals through their lifeworld. Subjecting these prejudices or traditions to analysis and bringing them to awareness functions to raise consciousness of the "choices" one makes that, prior to awareness, only seemed natural or inevitable.

Swing Voters as Audience

Prior to Election Day, voters assume the role of audience to (as opposed to participants in) a grand political pageant staged to persuade, dissuade, mobilize, and demobilize them. From the perspective of campaign practitioners, the primary role of the voter is to be subjected to as many messages as are affordable and efficacious. Putnam (2000) laments the role of the citizen as an election observer: "Now for almost all Americans, an election campaign is something that happens around us, a grating element in the background noise of everyday life, a fleeting image on a TV screen" (p. 41). At the level of a presidential election, however, this kind of detachment is almost unavoidable due to the virtual impossibility of a presidential candidate meeting even a fraction of voters. Mass communication is a necessity for candidates and the voters studied here are subjected to the complex environment it has helped forge; this environment includes televised and radio broadcast political advertisements, various forms of news, mailings, telephonic communication, billboards, yard-signs, and computer messages all supplemented by interpersonal communication (Pfau, Diedrich, Larson, & Van Winkle, 1995). It is impossible to study these voters without considering the environment to which they respond—anything else would be pure abstraction.

Describing the voter's environment this way is part of a gradual trend in mass communication research away from cause-and-effect models and strict sociological paradigms in exchange for the presumption of a culturally involved individual who plays an active role in determining meaning in his/her communication environment (e.g., Stern, 1994; Morgenstern, 1992). Nimmo and Sanders (1981) aptly outlined three stages through which mass communication research has progressed. Early studies were sociological, assuming that messages had mass effects (e.g., Cantril, Gaudet, & Herzog,

1940). This perspective is often termed the "Magic-bullet" paradigm, as it presumed messages were both uniform in content and effect (Shannon & Weaver, 1949). A message, properly "aimed," could "pierce" its target. Audiences according to this paradigm were passive vessels to be filled with messages. The researcher's job was to learn which demographics were influenced and why. This mode of research evolved into the "limited-effects" paradigm, a more social-psychological understanding of media's effects. This perspective evolved after effects researchers found little consistent or predictable results among the audiences they tested. Klapper (1960) argued that mass media functioned through a "nexus of mediating factors" (p. 8). Thus, limited-effects research developed, characterized by the attempts to predict receiver response by developing more complex models with growing numbers of antecedent variables. Research emphasis on antecedent variables has led to increased attention on the subject, making media research increasingly psychological. For example, uses and gratifications research turns the direction of research around, examining media effects from the audience's point of view, explaining what the audience does with the stimuli instead of the other way around (Katz & Lazarsfeld, 1955). Focus on the individual has made researchers increasingly aware that the meanings, and not just the effects, produced by advertisements and other forms of mass communication are contingent upon the individual.

The individual, however, does not have complete autonomy to construct the surrounding world as s/he pleases. Instead, as is suggested by phenomenology, the lifeworld that is synthesized and perceived by the individual is determined by cultural presuppositions—our horizons. The world as we know it is learned by engaging our cultural environment. Out of these engagements we develop unique horizons. Matters such as these were well understood by early researchers in this field. Campbell et al. (1960) write:

> If we are to understand what leads the voter to his decision at the polls we must know how he sees the things to which this decision relates. In casting a vote the individual acts toward a world of politics in which he perceives the personalities, issues, and the parties and other groupings of a presidential contest. His image of these matters may seem at times exceedingly ill-informed, but his behavior makes sense subjectively in terms of the way these political objects appear to him. (p. 42)

Although this project will problematize the notion of subjectivity, this book views the swing voter as an audience member in a complex "information environment" (Schudson, 1986). According to Schudson, the adult consumer of product advertising approaches messages with a lifetime of "informational resources" at his/her disposal. These resources shape meanings and make salient different facets of the messages they encounter.

Understanding swing voters as an audience embedded in both a culturally shared and individual history and as members of a complex information environment is precisely what campaign practitioners do (e.g., Packard, 1957; McGinniss, 1968; Schwartz, 1973; Sabato, 1981). Unfortunately, communication scholars primarily focus on the empirical characteristics and effects of political messages, namely, political advertisements. It is doubtless to me that effects research (Does advertisement X cause response Y?) is motivated by valid theoretical concerns. Nevertheless, the performance of this research tends to shed little on half of the transaction—the person sitting at home taking the messages in. It rarely takes into account meaningful differences between types of voters and the implications these differences may have for the interpretation of the stimuli the researchers use. Instead, scholars seem to prefer to rely on empirical presumptions, that a stimulus (usually a message in communication research) is monolithic, possessing one determinable meaning. Common sense, however, tells us that interpretation is always varied because it is filtered through the shared cultural and unique individual experiences, concerns, and anticipations of the interpreter.

If matters of interpretation were not important, campaign advisors would not put great efforts into learning the psychology of their target audiences. Campaigners know their audiences well, which is why questions and criticism about audience manipulation often arise among academics and political observers; some fear that campaigners can come to know the psychology of their audiences far better than they know themselves. Packard (1957) argued early that:

> All this probing and manipulation has its constructive and its amusing aspects; but also, I think it is fair to say, it has seriously antihumanistic implications. Much of it seems to represent regress rather than progress for man in his long struggle to become a rational and self-guiding being. (p. 6)

The fear, perhaps more valid today than ever, is that marketers could know their target audiences so well that they could cause people to base otherwise rational judgments on either emotional or subconscious processes. This concern is predicated on the argument that irrational political judgments are detrimental to democratic processes—a premise that I accept.

Schwartz (1973) complained that most voter research simply examined message understanding and retention. Although a great deal more advertising research has been conducted since Schwartz' *The Responsive Chord* was published, subsequent advertising and political advertising research typically suffers from similar limitations pandemic to positivistic methodologies; the presumed split between text and reader enables and limits scholars to measure what a receiver does with a message against what the message itself says. This perspective presupposes that the inherent meaning is explicit in a message. The researcher need only assume an objective or scientific standpoint to be qualified to conduct this research. Research of this kind is remarkable both for its volume as well as for what it ignores—meaning.

The notion that meaning is contingent upon cultural presuppositions, experiences, and context is derived from phenomenology and is well applied to culture by Hall (1973). He explains that the meanings that people educe are built upon the order or structure that *they* give to stimuli. These orders are different among cultures and among people.

> Groups can be defined by the relation of their members to a certain pattern. The individuals of a group share patterns that enable them to see the same thing and this holds them together. (Hall, 1973, p. 125)

This runs counter to the often-held assumption that two people encountering the same phenomena will experience the same thing, if all external states can be adequately controlled. This assumption is inaccurate, because what stands out as meaningful to each person is based upon the order given the phenomena by cultural imperatives (c.f., Goffman, 1974). Hall's (1973) emphasis on the value of learning about the assumptions of one's own culture is relevant here, because knowledge of the way swing voters perceive elections may shed light on different modes of reading and different grounds for making sense of political information.

With specific regard to political advertising, Schwartz (1973) addresses the role that context plays in the development and audience interpretation of political spots. He explains, "good political research seeks out attitudes in the environment and then judges a political spot by the way it affects these attitudes" (p. 100). That this needed to be written at all is surprising to contemporary advertising audiences who find this observation elementary. Quite simply, Schwartz is describing the role context plays in the meaning and impact of a spot. West (1993) also maintains that political advertising cannot be understood without attention to context. Context influences the person who ultimately produces the meaning of the spot: the spot's saliencies, the weighted relevance of issues, images, and values. Key (1966) addressed this matter well before televised political advertising assumed its central role in the contemporary campaign:

> Differences in voters' interest, in their range of information, in the orientation of their attention, in their firsthand experience, and in their exposure to communications produce enormous variation in their perceptions of events and, consequently, in their appraisals of the alternatives posed by the electoral system. The explanation of voting behavior requires estimation of the modal parameters of the perceptions of the political world to which voters respond, a task to which insufficient resources have been devoted. (p. 110)

It is the constantly changing context, environment, individual priorities, and circumstances for individuals and groups that ultimately comprise the situations in which voters make up their minds (Campbell, Converse, Miller, & Stokes, 1960). As a component of the election context, the meanings of political spots are also influenced by context.

There is considerable reason to believe that campaign practitioners view context, text, and reader as components of the meanings of advertisements. Schwartz (1973) states outright that "the people listening are actually part of the content of the advertisement" (p. 101). Thus, it is concluded here that there exists an overwhelming and much neglected need to research the interaction between voters and advertisers from a perspective consistent with Schwartz (1973) and others—a hermeneutic perspective.

Political Communication Environment

In this book I argue that swing voters are both a product of and producers of a unique and shared cultural predisposition toward presidential voting. Shaped by numerous forces including the political information environment, attitudes about the nature of democracy and truth, severe time demands experienced by the typical voter and the ways with which we use what is available, analysis of swing voter discourse provides us with a way to understand the conventions used by them to cope with the task of voting for president.

The typical voter is flooded with information about candidates and campaigns. Pfau et al. (1995) cite newspapers, television news, televised speeches, televised interviews, television advertisements, televised debates, as well as interpersonal communication among the most influential sources of information about candidates. This short list excludes radio news and radio spots as well as countless other modes utilized by campaigns to communicate with voters, including phone banks, literature drops, yard signs, billboards, "coffees" (modernized by Howard Dean's "meet-ups") and automated phone message machines that leave seemingly personalized messages from the presidential candidate on workers' answering machines during the afternoon hours. Typically the tape-recorded candidate expresses regret for having missed you during this call. Those lucky enough to be home for the call are greeted by a swift click, because the machine placing the call hangs up only to call later in a repeated attempt to reach its actual target—the answering machine.

Making sense of this volume of messages and information is not a simple task and it isn't likely to become simpler as campaign practitioners continue to adopt practices pioneered by product advertisers in their pursuit of consumer "mind share" (Mills, 2001). For instance, Bagdikian (1997) explains that mass mediated advertising for election contests are influenced by the shapes and sizes of media markets, forcing candidates to standardize, broadly cast, and make their arguments less specific. Schuessler (2000) maintains that broadcast and mass-marketed campaigns result in an "all-things-to-all-people strategy" that focuses less on policy and more on symbol-intensive imagery (pp. 87–88). Meanwhile, the Internet as well as satellite and cable television channels have increased the ability of campaigns to nimbly narrow-cast tailored messages to specific demographic groups who possess their own unique anxieties.

Surprisingly, the coping mechanisms developed by swing voters to manage this aggressive and rich information environment lend little support to the characterizations of contemporary voters as cynical (e.g., Hart, 1999) and disengaged (e.g., Berger, 2000). Though their daily behavior may allude to a disinterest, to the extent that swing voters vote, they are neither cynical nor disengaged. Instead, it is maintained that they are differently engaged: engaged in ways many scholars aren't equipped to appreciate because of the limitations of the perspectives and models used to anticipate and understand voter behavior. Though these voters may be nonpartisan, this is not their defining characteristic; how they vote is not a function of partisanship because partisanship is disregarded by these voters altogether. It is more accurate to characterize these voters as individualistic by default. Eschewing partisan identification or other group identifications, these concerned voters find themselves without much ground with which to make their decisions. The typical decision made by the participants in this study was formulated at the last minute. The voter based his/her choice on the candidate perceived to best help the voter with his/her immediate and concrete needs. Excluded from their reasoning were more abstract concerns such as those related to community or social obligations.

Analysis of the data collected here indicates several more specific characteristics of the swing voter as s/he copes with the task of voting in our culture. The presumption in their approach to voting is that an ideal candidate exists. Consistent with the premises of rationality, which maintain that transcendental truths can be found or approximated, the swing voter proceeds from the assumption that the right candidate among those in the field can and should be determined. Choosing the right candidate, they believe, is simply a matter of devoting oneself to studying the available material sufficiently until this candidate is unmistakably obvious. As a result, swing voters profess to highly value information. Both quality and quantity of information constitute the criteria by which swing voters assess candidates and their messages.

Unfortunately, this set of assumptions sets up an impossible standard for voter decision making because the amount of information available to voters is immeasurable. Voluminous sums of information coupled with severe limits in available time (Schor, 1991) to process it ultimately leaves the swing voter frustrated and incapable of discerning the ideal candidate. Belated commitment to any candidate seems to be the result of these pressures. Swing voters are found to distribute positive and negative criticisms evenly between the candidates and doing so is perceived by them as fair. Only rarely is praise or criticism distributed inequitably between them. Without "sufficient" information or partisanship as a guide, as perceived by the interviewees, these swing voters were found to make last-minute decisions based upon their own immediate self-interests.

And why not, considering the tremendous time constraints placed on the daily lives of individuals in the political system of the United States? The aforementioned assertions maintain that swing voters exhibit in their talk evidence of conscientiousness and rationality with respect to voting. Rarely, however, are they credited by the voices of our culture with such attributes. A probable reason for this is the obtuse assumption that because "dumbed down" political messages work, voters must be dullards incapable or unwilling to devote themselves to sufficient research or reasoning. It is argued here that this perspective fails to take the lifeworld of the voter into consideration. I am not suggesting that laziness on the part of voters is warranted: Instead, what a voter considers sound reason can vary according to the demands placed upon her/him. In an effort to live one's life in a culture characterized as "time famished" (Johnson, 1978), reliance upon political advertisements makes sense as media spots—including Web, TV, radio, newspapers—equip the voter with valuable heuristic tools with which to make decisions. Ethical and information-driven advertising can provide voters with much needed information (if voters' lifestyles preclude them from researching the candidates) when delivered in the multimedia formats appropriate to the many lifestyles found in our communities.

It certainly is not argued in this book that swing voters are insufficiently rational. What is found in the voters' talk described in Chapter 3 is support for Popkin's (1991) description of "low-information reasoning." He explains that low-information reasoning is "by no means devoid of substantive content, but is instead a process that economically incorporates learning and information from past experiences, daily life, the media, and political campaigns" (p. 212). Just what a *sufficiently* reasoned voter is, is not clear. Any person's decision is ultimately going to be contingent upon his or her vantage point. That swing voters are motivated enough to vote and concerned enough to devote effort to considering the merits of the candidates at all is commendable and makes their participation valuable to the deliberative process. Their reasoning hardly warrants criticism as long as we take into account the quality of the information used and manner of its delivery.

Consistent with Popkin (1991), Downs (1957) argues that voters make rational decisions, but that their desire to be rational competes with other needs, including time costs. A voter is rational if his/her efforts to obtain information are useful "for making decisions which will help bring about the social state which he (sic) most prefers" (p. 213). In this process, time is the "main scarce resource consumed" (p. 209). How does this apply to voters that have precious little time to invest in candidate research? Downs explains that this condition does not matter, for even choosing to vote is rational if the result of *not* voting is believed to contribute to a less appealing society.

> The advantage of voting per se is that it makes democracy possible. If no one votes, then the system collapses because no government is chosen. We assume that the citizens of a democracy subscribe to its principles and therefore derive benefits from its continuance; hence they do not want it to collapse. For this reason they attach value to the act of voting per se, and receive a return from it. (pp. 261-261)

This perception challenges the idea held by many that these types of voters probably should not vote because their vote has not been sufficiently reasoned. Criticism of this sort certainly emerges from a privileged vantage point characterized by the presumption of temporal bounty.

In addition to dealing with time constrictions, the horizons of contemporary voters in the United States are, in part, constituted by modern notions of individuality. The notion of *public* is in disarray. Today's voter finds him/herself in a cultural milieu that values individualism or perspectivism, which is to say that the ego is valued over larger social relationships and responsibilities (Gebser, 1949/1985). Our democratic mode of governance, our voting procedures, and the way swing voters vote are manifestations of this horizon. Although perspectivism made democratic governance possible, another apparent manifestation of perspectival consciousness among swing voters is reduced concern for a greater whole—atomism. Individuals perceive themselves as abstracted from their immediate community and the public and the shared responsibilities that accompany community. This is not to claim that these voters are value free—otherwise they would have little reason to vote. Although swing voters clearly value voting and participation, this is seen as an ends and not a means; put simply, it is believed that voting helps the democratic system while not voting harms it. However, with growing suspicion of and/or irrelevance of partisanship and little consistent ideological ground with which to use to help shape decisions, swing voters ultimately rely upon the only concrete matter of concern—the self and its immediate needs. Consequently, it is important for the swing voter to vote, yet how they vote is governed almost completely by self concerns. The swing voter's final decision is not the outcome of a rational process of determining the ideal candidate according to any criteria characterized by concern for a larger community, something like a party platform, for instance. Instead, the swing voter compromises some purer notion of rationality by voting for the best candidate believed to provide the most immediate return. Such an approach shouldn't be too surprising considering the large number of messages trumpeted at voters, the limited quality and depth of information in those messages, the available time with which to process them, and the political pre-understandings and cultural attitudes discussed later in Chapters 4, 5, and 6.

2

DISCUSSION OF METHOD

> We are "thrown" into the world as beings who understand and interpret—so if we are to understand what it is to be human beings, we must seek to understand understanding itself, in its rich, full, and complex dimensions.
> R. J. Bernstein (1983)

In this project I approach swing voters with the assumption that their attitudes are products of an information environment unique to the United States and its political campaigns. I begin by asking, "Who are swing voters?" in order to offer an answer that sheds light on the swing voters' general approach to presidential voting. Though this project was originally an attempt to understand how swing voters made sense of political advertisements, as the project developed, I soon realized that a different understanding was emerging. Voters would barely respond to the specific advertisements that they were shown. Instead, they shared a great deal about their political attitudes regarding presidential politics and campaigns. Significant themes emerged in the discussions and a more general impression regarding the nature of these voters unfolded.

The method of analysis took me in a surprising direction. Explaining how this happened is simple. First, good qualitative research often makes unanticipated discoveries. Resistance to unexpected outcomes amounts to little more than a self-fulfilling prophecy—nothing more than fitting square pegs into round holes. Once a person or a team of researchers focuses efforts exclusively on one phenomenon, they should expect to encounter phenomena that were less apparent than before they began. Second, this project is exploratory in nature; as such, it is not guided by any particular political theory, voting theory, mass communication theory, or otherwise. I did not begin this project with the intention of testing a hypothesis or to replicate prior research. With regard to the subject matter studied in this project, there is such an enormous deficit in the research that there exist too few testable presumptions about swing voters. There does not appear to be any theory regarding swing voters anywhere. Third, and in accordance with the goals outlined here, the methods of data collection and analysis described at length in this section were chosen for the purposes of exploration. By bracketing presumptions about what one may find, as is the goal with ethnography and hermeneutics, the researcher is equipped to acknowledge unexpected outcomes.

As a result, this project is "guided" by an open-ended research question. The researcher does not ask if swing voters interpret campaign communication this way or that way. Instead, it is asked, "How do they?" How do swing voters make sense of messages tailored for their consumption? How do they manage the flood of information? *Do* they manage this flood? As of yet, very little formal study along these lines has been conducted, and thus there is little theory available to guide it. That the focus of this project changed significantly makes evident that the nature of the research question did not limit what was observed and concluded.

The previous chapter explained the meaning of *swing voter*. As operationalized in this study, they are individuals who self-identified themselves as having waited until the final weekend of the 2000 presidential campaign to make their voting decisions. Equally important, however, is understanding whether these individuals constitute a cultural phenomenon (a group) worth studying from an ethnographic perspective. I obviously now believe swing voters constitute something unique; they share political attitudes. This conclusion, however, was not quite as clear until after the study was underway because the group had not previously been formally subjected to investigation. What criteria did this group satisfactorily meet in order for them to be considered a cultural phenomenon? The answer to this question depends on the definition of culture. As Geertz (1973) points out, the term *culture* is used often and vaguely enough as to be nearly meaningless. In his approach to ethnography, *culture*

> ... denotes an historically transmitted pattern of meanings embodied in symbols, a system of inherited conceptions expressed in symbolic forms by means of which men communicate, perpetuate, and develop their knowledge about and attitudes toward life. (p. 89)

Thus, we could expect varied modes of understanding among cultures within a culture. In much the same way that Culler (1982) identified various ways of "Reading as a Woman," this project presupposed that different ways of reading political messages could potentially emerge among different communities. But is a group of voters characterized by when, in relation to election day, they made their voting decisions? Do swing voters possess their own unique symbols, knowledge, and attitudes? Some maintain that, if they do, then these voters are, instead, a subculture, possessing "a set of shared symbolic ideas held by a collectivity within a larger society" (Gudykunst & Kim, 1997). Use of this terminology is fair enough except that "subculture" connotes discreteness. I *can* visit a place where discrete populations such as Mexican-Americans, Jewish-Americans, or football players gather, but the same is not true for swing voters. Swing voters appear to be scattered throughout society. For the purposes of this study, swing voters are considered a "cultural phenomenon" characterized by their unique "read" of the United States political scene but not so easily identified by any sort of demographic characteristic.

How then can swing voters possess a shared understanding of anything? In a sense, it is argued here that U.S. citizens are taught, or socialized, to read messages. This education is both formal and informal. Institutions vital to political socialization help swing voters develop their own way of making campaign communication meaningful and relevant. Formally, young people learn how to identify relevant issues and understand their historical situatedness from community institutions. Less formally, voters learn ways of managing the political environment. Although schools instruct us in, perhaps, the higher standards to which voters should aspire, the private experiences of family, friends, work, and television teach (or reinforce) complementary and alternative ways of organizing and attributing meaning to the myriad political messages in our environment. These multiple influences shape how Republicans, Democrats, Independents, disengaged voters, and swing voters learn to "read" politics. Swing voters are distinguished from other groups by virtue of the conventions applied when interpreting these messages.

Inasmuch as this project is examining the conventions by which meaning is attributed by swing voters, it could be said that it is guided by structuralist presuppositions. Strictly in the sense that Culler (1982) uses the term, this would be correct: most structuralists presuppose that interpretation is not exclusively determined by the text and the cultural codes required to access them. It is more accurate, however, to consider this project guided by philosophical hermeneutics (Gadamer, 1977). According to structuralism, culturally determined codes are employed by readers to make meaning of texts. This is not to say that once the text is engaged, codes are used to make sense of it. Instead, it is maintained that the text *cannot* be engaged without some familiarity with these codes. One is either equipped with codes with which to access the text or not. Moreover, text does not have a monolithic meaning. Although the text may have an intended meaning, and may inherently possess a specific meaning, depending upon the conventions with which the reader engages the text, a different meaning may be produced by the reader. The reader may negotiate a meaning or develop an oppositional reading. Culler (1982) explains that the latter can be developed in response to the text's perceived meaning. In any case, the interpretation is a response to the text's inherent meaning to the extent that this meaning can be ascertained by the reader.

The approach used here to understand swing voters is more accurately termed hermeneutic: in keeping with the phenomenological tradition, hermeneutics collapses the distinction between subject and object (reader and text). Distinctions between structuralism and post-structuralism are inadequate for understanding relationships between reader and text because each privileges text or reader. Philosophical hermeneutics privileges neither text nor reader. No meaning would exist without the horizons of both the text and reader encountering and fusing with one another. The reader in this scenario, from the hermeneutic point of view, is not subjective. Born to personal experiences as well as shared historical horizons from which the culture's linguistic traditions emerge, the meanings reasonably assigned to any given phenomenon are limited (some are reasonable and some are not). The individual reader does not have some radical freedom with which to create a new meaning from a text unless it is in *response* to some culturally derived understanding of the text—which is not to suggest that the text has a monolithic meaning. For example, one cannot watch an episode of *Friends* and be justifiably pleased with believing they have just seen the latest installment of *Who Wants to Be a Millionaire*. To do so would be to create a new text altogether, and might also require a visit with a therapist.

On the other hand, the text is not an object that speaks for itself or has "being-in-itself" (Gadamer, 1960/2000, p. 476). Both the world and texts are mediated through language. As such, neither can be known in a way that transcends the limits of human means for engaging these phenomena. Presuming the world-as-object can be engaged and measured without the distorting limitations (the modern language that I use hesitantly) of human understanding is an abstraction, a prejudice of the modern/scientific vantage point.

> The objectifying procedures of natural science and the concept of being-in-itself, which is intended in all knowledge, proved to be an abstraction when viewed from the medium that language is.

> Abstracted from the fundamental relation to the world that is given in the linguistic nature of our experience of it, science attempts to become certain about entities by methodically organizing its knowledge of the world. Consequently it condemns as heresy all knowledge that does not allow of this kind of certainty and that therefore cannot serve the growing domination of being. By contrast, we have endeavored to liberate the mode of being of art and history, and the experience corresponding to them, from the ontological prejudice implied in the ideal of scientific objectivity; and, in the view of the experience of art and history, we were led to a universal hermeneutics that was concerned with the general relationship of man to the world. (Gadamer, 1960/2000, p. 276)

Gadamer's philosophy re-evaluates the notion of "truth." A "right" or "true" meaning is determined neither by the text nor the reader. The text would be senseless without the foreground or horizon of the interpreter. Nevertheless, the reader must approach the text as though it has a true meaning; after all, it has its own horizon. To the extent that the reader's history is always accruing, there can never be just one read. "True" meaning is indeterminable though approachable and worthy of pursuit. Truth, with respect to meaning, has been taken back from the natural sciences by Gadamer and other like-minded individuals. It is no longer limited to the realm of methodologically verifiable concepts. This was Gadamer's critique of method: it presumed that one epistemology (modern/scientific) was superior to alternatives that were best fit for understanding human social phenomena (aesthetic knowledge and historic knowledge).

Utilizing a philosophical hermeneutic perspective, this study acknowledges that the codes utilized to understand messages are not deterministic. There exists "room" within which one can negotiate and resist meanings but this also assumes some understanding of the text to which the reader offers resistance. Moreover, the context in which future elections occur will change. In light of new information and dynamics, perceived options available to the voter in the information environment will change. "Cultural theory is of and *makes* culture. . . . Reading explanations and description creates new relationships in the world of the reader." (Kramer, 1992, pp. 31–32). Conclusions found in this book are not considered fixed or nomothetic. Instead, the following arguments regarding swing voter understandings contribute to the milieu in which future elections will hold meaning.

What follows is a brief look at some of the limitations of other methods currently being applied to the study of voters. This provides the ground upon which the specific method employed here is described and justified, including a discussion of data collection, participant recruitment, and interview design. The method of analysis is described followed by a discussion of validity.

LIMITATIONS OF NATURAL SCIENCE METHODOLOGY

Method is discussed here, though not for the standard scientific reasons of facilitating replication. Although replicability would certainly lend a great deal of credibility to the findings here, it is not believed that the results discussed here can be replicated. There are no controls on the phenomena. Subsequent researchers cannot go back in time and replicate the conditions and attitudes of the time in question. The 2000 presidential election has come and gone. Instead, the method employed is explained as a matter of record. Curious readers should know how the study was conducted as each facet of the approach is part of the overall argument made here; the care taken in compiling the data used is a fair estimate of the overall validity of the claims that follow. I am not under the impression that the method for collecting data was designed perfectly, or that the design did not ultimately influence the results in any way. It is maintained, however, that great care was taken and that the results possess validity and social value.

Nevertheless, scholarly research of both voters and political communication is often based on the premises and practices of the natural science paradigm, which presumes that experience is objective, measurable, and testable and that conditions, factors, and variables can be controlled and manipulated. Good social or human science acknowledges the differences in how these presumptions apply to itself as compared with the natural sciences. Hesse (1980) argues that "In human science data are not detachable from theory, for what count as data are often determined in the light of some theoretical interpretation" (p. 170). Although arguments like these have ironically begun to influence the natural sciences, social science research, despite its more obvious limitations, is still being conducted according to the dictates of empirical natural science.

> The assumption has been that the social sciences differ in the degree and not in kind from the natural sciences and that ideally the methods and standards appropriate to the natural sciences can be extended by analogy to the social sciences. (Bernstein, 1983 p. 32)

These practices are applied in the research described hereafter. These examples illustrate some of the standard limitations of adhering to natural science dictates when conducting social science investigations.

In her survey of political communication research and issues, Kaid's (1981) summary of the discipline evidences a natural-science fixation on the requirements of logical empiricism. Namely, she is concerned with metrics. She explains that survey research "on political advertising continues to suffer from weak measures of receiver exposure." Reliance upon voter recall is termed "a particularly defective measuring device." She recommends the use of audimeters (hand held dials) to "allow more accurate measures" of audience exposure. Field experiments, she explains, fail to "isolate important variables" reducing its ability to "ensure valid results." Stimulus material is considered "poor and unrealistic." To overcome some of the validity problems with which political communication research is faced, she recommends careful measure of galvanic skin response, brain waves, eye movement, pupil dilation, and so on. She adds that external validity would be enhanced by conducting more research on subjects other than college students.

When we look at specific studies, we find that, to some extent, these types of recommendations are attended to. Unfortunately, the latter recommendation pertaining to research subjects relates to a significant inadequacy in many media-effects studies. *Audience* is often treated as a monolithic entity. Subject pools are frequently aggregates of conveniently recruited respondents (e.g., undergraduates at a large southeastern university); typically, little concern is exhibited for fundamental differences inherent in the group. Certainly scholars do not believe that campaign communication audiences are homogeneous, yet their research often fails to reflect the sensitivity to audience utilized by campaign practitioners. For example, Kaid (1997) conducted a study that measured the effect of political spots on the assessment of presidential candidate images. The subjects she employed included 604 college students in one leg of the study, and another 525 college students in a second leg. The results of the interactions between the students and the stimuli were broken down according to sex and party affiliation (Democrat, Republican, and Independent). Not only are these divisions arbitrary (imposed without any tested explanation of the relationship between affiliation and interpretation), they are potentially meaningless altogether. First, the author fails to provide any theoretical explication for why the sample is divided according to sex and party. Do women react differently to political advertisements than do men? Moreover, what constitutes a Democrat in this instance is determined by self-report, which would not necessarily be a problem if the participants had any voting record on which to base their assessment. Though we are not given the mean age of the participants, we can reasonably expect the mean to lie somewhere between 18 and 25. Considering that the study was done just prior to the 1996 election, it is safe to estimate that most participants had likely never before voted for president. Do individuals with little or no prior political experience react to political spots in a fashion that is similar to those to whom the spots are targeted? What does it mean to a first-time voter when s/he identifies her/himself as an Independent, Democrat, or Republican? It is an important question, and the significance of Kaid's (1997) study depended on some exploration of these issues, unless of course the researcher presumed little or no variance in interpretation of the messages among the study's participants.

In the previous case, the effect of the nature of televisual messages was in question. The following study examines the effects of traditional versus nontraditional forms of media on the attitudes of voters and evidences the value of measurement at the expense of theory. McLeod et al. (1996) specifically tried to understand what "kinds of people" used traditional and nontraditional forms of political information. In a sense, these researchers are performing ethnography through metrics; which is to say that they are not learning much about the "kinds of people" at all. Relying on data-mining, they look to see if numerous antecedents (including political interest, ideology, and party affiliation) and consequences (including campaign interest, participation, vote likelihood, and affect) correlated with the use of either type of information. In this case, no theoretical presuppositions are used to help make sense of the data. Instead, it is presumed, based upon the rules of stochastics, that different phenomena would not correlate unless there was some inherent and meaningful link between them. Given this logic, it might be interesting to understand why Elizabeth Taylor's divorces correlated with stock market surges (it is doubtful that this can be explained theoretically) (Jensen, 2000). In the end, we learn little about the different "kinds" of people, other than that the types of information consumed have the greatest "influences" on more labile characteristics of voters' attitudes.

The next study provides theoretical explication for the testing conducted and gives some reason for exclusively including college students as respondents. In this case, however, we see strict adherence to metrics coupled with the complete abstraction of the study from an election context. Austin and Pinkleton (1995) administered a survey to 257 college students in the fall of 1991, nearly a year away from the next presidential election. Their goal was to measure, among other things, how attitudes like negativism, cynicism, and apathy related to voting intent among "less experienced eligible voters" (p. 215). If Wattenberg's (1991) conclusions are accurate, voter perceptions of candidates drive presidential elections. When the study was conducted, however, the democratic candidate was not yet known, and the incumbent president was sitting on a 73% approval rating (Kagay, 1991). This changed significantly by the winter of that year, with Bush garnering only 51% approval by December. By election day of 2002, Bush could only attract 38% of the vote (Toner, 1992), and the percentage of the youth vote participating was at its highest since 1972 (Federal Election Commission, 2003). Their study regarding the relationships between attitudes and voting intent was couched in an anomalous context characterized by incumbent disenchantment, sweeping poll shifts, viable third-party candidates, and unprecedented participation among younger voters. Moreover, their operationalization of "less experienced voter" ignored older citizens who had never voted in the past, new citizens, or voters who had taken a break from voting. Austin and Pinkleton (1995) succeed in highlighting the complex relationships between the attitudes they discuss and voting behavior, yet their approach offers little real world insight into the impact of these attitudes on actual elections.

These studies provide a fair sampling of the types of research conducted and published in this field. Typically, scholars try to isolate components of the linear communication model (Shannon and Weaver, 1949) and study them for their influence on the outcomes of elections (effects). Within their linear framework of communication, it is often understood that the context within which communication occurs can have significant influences on the meanings and outcomes of the exchange. However, when sufficient controls cannot be placed on the variables influencing communication, researchers often make do with what they have, which is to say, they resign themselves to controlling very little. Moreover, a lack of control is always introduced into a study when human subjects are involved. How the message is decoded varies: herein lies a problem with the use of Shannon and Weaver's (1949) communication model; it wasn't intended to explain *human* communication, so it fails to account for interpretation variance. There is no doubt that social science scholars are attempting to perform the best science. However, given the vast number of variables that fall outside the realm of what the researcher can anticipate and control, readers should expect the conclusions to contain more qualifiers than they typically do. At times, the inability to control context or environment is considered virtuous because the study was conducted "in the field," suggesting the results possess *more* validity. On the other hand, when the researcher is aspiring to achieve some generalizability, she/he attempts to control as much as possible. Although the standards for control set by natural sciences are rarely met in the social sciences, some research still implies that by virtue of the utilization of empirical methodology, researchers have tapped nomothetic laws and are justified in making apodictic claims.

METHODOLOGY

As suggested by the discussion of ethnography and hermeneutics, the method employed for the collection of data in this study is significantly different from the methods employed in the aforementioned studies. There were two concerns with conducting the study. First, I needed data that reflected a reaction to political communication: I was concerned with giving respondents an opportunity to just "interact" with televised political spots. Although studying the recollections and perceptions of the 2000 presidential campaign and its spots would have been somewhat enlightening, it was doubtful that the spots would have been fresh enough in their minds for respondents to give accurate and vivid reactions to them. Second, I needed to interact with the subjects involved to help develop the insights into their reactions to political communication and voting in general. The design reflects the intent of this study to shed light on the interpretation of political spots. Ultimately, the interactions with the subjects expanded the project, providing insights into attitudes about all sorts of political communiqués.

The method employed to evoke swing voters' reactions of political communication (namely televised political spots) was patterned after a method of analysis used to develop Louise Rosenblatt's (1978) reader's response theory of literary interpretation. Reader's response theory was developed from interviews Rosenblatt conducted with her undergraduate students designed to elicit the "paths by which students approached . . . a tentative first interpretation" of a text (p. 7). Rosenblatt's (1978) approach is significant for *several* reasons. First, in keeping with philosophical hermeneutics (though this wasn't her intent), she grants outright that multiple interpretations of text are not only possible but are simply the nature of interpretation. If neither the text nor the reader dictates what is true meaning, then multiple valid interpretations are possible. Second, the latter point implies (though she is more explicit) Rosenblatt's acknowledgment that meaning is created in the meeting of text and reader. This recognizes the role of subjectivity in determine meaning, a role that is denied by more static positivistic conceptualizations of communication. Critiques of her theory's emphasis upon the subjective are incomplete and miss the point. Even seemingly "objective" interpretations come from somewhere—some shared perspective.

The method used by Rosenblatt in developing her approach is not fully articulated in her work partly, it seems, because it was developed over many years of instruction. Her research was done informally. She explains that she presented written texts (e.g., poems and books) to her students and instructed them to write down their own thoughts about the meaning of the text as this meaning came to them. The thoughts of hundreds of subjects were collected and analyzed over a number of years.

The method of analysis Rosenblatt (1978) used appears to have been liberated from any natural science systematization, though this is not to say her work is not rigorous. Instead, the method of analysis seems ethnographic in nature. Her objective is to explain the essential dynamics of the reading process. Her conclusions make clear her goal of developing a theory of interpretation with epistemological ground consistent with her rejection of Cartesian dualism. She finds support for her conclusions in the analysis of student interactions over many years. Rosenblatt (1978) maintains that the meanings developed by readers are contingent and can by no means be subjective *or* objective.

> As with all texts, the reader must bring a whole body of cultural assumptions, practical knowledge, awareness of literary conventions, readiness to think and feel. These provide the basis for weaving a meaningful structure around the clues offered by the verbal symbols. (p. 88)

The following project incorporates Rosenblatt's epistemological presuppositions into the investigations of the cultural assumptions and practical knowledge of a specific group of readers—swing voters.

The following paragraphs describe and offer justification for the specific method used in the analysis of swing voters' interactions with political communication. An approach identified here as ethnographic interviewing is utilized involving analysis of two types of data: written reactions to political spots and interviews. Informants were sampled according to a purposive scheme (chosen to fit a profile) and asked to view political spots from the 2000 presidential election. The method of data analysis shares with the ethnographic approach its goal to represent in writing the cultural assumptions of a community (Van Maanen, 1988) and to search for and sort emergent structures of signification (Geertz, 1973).

Informants

Good social science research pays careful attention to the sample used. This is true because the laws of stochastics dictate that, for research results to be generalizable, a sample has to be randomly selected from the population under investigation. This study does not maintain that its results are generalizable on the basis of its adhering to stochastic rules. Nevertheless, great care is taken in choosing participants such that it can be best argued that the conclusions are argumentatively sound. The following short discussion provides a rationale for both the number and types of subjects to be included in the project.

As noted, little consistent social science research has been devoted to understanding swing voters as an audience. Moreover, the notion of "swing voter" has never been well-defined or consistently operationalized; for these reasons the study is exploratory. Given the methods employed for this type of study, the purposive method of sampling is ideal; this sampling method ensures the participation of a broad and representative sample. The sample is representative to the extent that demographic groups that constitute swing voters were included. At the same time, this sampling method avoids the pitfalls of a pure convenience sample. Mead (1953) explains the relative merits of this approach:

> The validity of the sample depends not so much upon the number of cases as upon the proper specification of the informant, so that he or she can be accurately placed in terms of a very large number of variables. . . . Within this extensive degree of specification, each informant is studied as a perfect example, an organic representation of his complete cultural experience. (p. 646)

Each subject is viewed as one rich empirical example.

This project is governed by rules that enable the researcher to dig deeply into individual cases, looking less for the distribution of characteristics that reflect the greater population. As a result, the sample is not nearly as large as is typical for social science research. Morse (1994) contends that sufficient sampling for interviews (like ethnographic interviews) is determined by "indices of saturation, such as repetition in the information obtained and confirmation of previously collected data" (p. 230). The sample size for this study was governed by saturation or repetition of the themes that emerged from interviews, sample representativeness, and the quality of the interview. The latter concern led to the exclusion of four interviews, with a total sample size amounting to thirty interviewees. Although I pursued a diverse group of people in order to increase the likelihood of encountering different responses and attitudes, themes began to repeat early in the process.

The population of swing voters was found to be very diverse during the 2000 election; no one demographic group dominated. The Pew Research Center (Kohut, 2000) conducted an extensive pre-election poll during November 2000 from the second through the fifth consisting of 1,829 interviews conducted over the telephone. Respondents were randomly selected among registered voters nationwide. This data provides demographic proportions of committed Gore, Bush, and swing voters during this time period. The characteristics of the population reflected in their survey functioned as a guide for this project's sampling. From this data, a carefully developed purposive stratified sampling method was used to avoid neglecting the potential variance among these voters.

The Pew Research Center data (Kohut, 2000) was used to determine the prominent characteristics of swing voters to be included in this study's sample. These characteristics were figured by comparing the relative population sizes of swing voters to committed voters among different demographic groups. In other words, subjects were deliberately sampled from the demographic groups that possessed significant differences between swing voters and committed voters, as ascertained with z-tests. For example, 10% of swing voters identified themselves as African American, whereas only 2% of voters committed to then-governor Bush identified themselves as African American. These groups are significantly different from what we would expect if distribution of these populations was governed by chance. For this reason, I was certain to include African Americans in the sample. As a result of these measures the sample reflects the sundry social and economic influences that shape this population. The advantage of this approach is that it provided opportunities for different perspectives within the population to emerge, increasing the likelihood that the different attitudes existing among this population would have a chance to arise during the interviewing process.

Table 2.1 identifies six swing voter demographic groups possessing differences from Bush and Gore voters. These groups were pursued during the recruitment stage of the study. For the purposes of recruiting subjects, swing voters were considered individuals who voted and made their decisions relatively late in the campaign, seemingly because they could not decide among the options. Recruits were screened with the following two questions:

1. Did you vote in the last presidential election?
2. How long before election day did you choose for whom to vote?

Table 2.1.

Demographic	Significant Differences with z-Scores
Race	African American swing 10% > African American Bush 2% ($z = 5.89$)
Sex	Female swing 53% > Female Bush 45% ($z = 2.35$)
Age	35-44 swing 24% > 35-44 Gore 18% ($z = 2.41$)
	45-54 swing 24% > 45-54 Bush 18% ($z = 2.23$)
Income	$20-$30G swing 12% > $20-$30G Bush 8% ($z = 2.31$)
Education	H.S./GED swing 41% > H.S./GED Bush 26% ($z = 4.68$)
	H.S./GED swing 41% > H.S./GED Gore 31% ($z = 3.18$)
	Vo./Tech swing 6% > Vo./Tech. Gore 3% ($z = 2.00$)
Ethnicity Hispanic/Spanish)	Hispanic swing 9% > Hispanic Bush 4% ($z = 3.1$)

Most people interviewed responded to the latter question with some variant of "in the voting booth," though any voter stating they chose their candidate no earlier than the weekend before the election (November 3, 2000) was asked to participate.

It was important for me to help ensure the validity of this study by avoiding a convenient sample of undergraduate students. I am convinced that if I had resigned myself to recruiting university students, I could have finished recruiting and interviewing within a month. Instead, recruitment took three months, and the interviewing, which involved travel and missed and rescheduled appointments, took more than four months. Though a small number of participants were solicited from an Illinois public university, once a sufficient number of that cohort was interviewed, advertisements were placed in newspapers throughout Chicagoland (the *Chicago Tribune* and *The Reader*) to recruit individuals for different segments of the profile. Additionally, subjects were recruited from assisted-living communities, fire departments, community colleges (known to have more nontraditional college demographics than is traditionally true for universities), and community bingos. In some instances, the snowball technique was utilized, as subjects referred me to other individuals qualified to participate. In one instance, a woman playing bingo laughed as I was screening her and told me to interview her husband. She invited me to call their home the next day and arrange to interview him, providing me with one of the richer interviews.

Subject Profile

The demographic questionnaires were used to develop a description of the subjects participating in the study. Nearly all of the desired demographic groups are represented in the sample. Both African American and Latino voters each constitute 8% of the sample. The sex of the sample was somewhat evenly split, with women comprising 57% of the sample. The ages ranged from 18 to 80, while the average age was 37. Both age groups of particular interest were included in the sample: The group consisting of ages 35 to 44 made up 40% of those interviewed, while the 45 to 54 year old group constituted 23% of the sample. The average income of respondents was $56,764. Finding individuals with income between $20,000 and $30,000 per year was difficult for a number of reasons. Primarily, the median household income in Chicago's county, Cook, lies between $44,618 and $55,320, while the median for the surrounding suburbs lies between $59,351 and $67,887 (U.S. Census Bureau, 2001). Though the average for the sample is somewhat high, relative to the nation's median of $41,994, it is close to the median of the community from which subjects were recruited. Any concerns about the extent to which the sample is representative need to be tempered with an awareness that younger respondents cited their parents' household income. This may have skewed the numbers. It should be noted that a large proportion of the sample met the education goals. Most had a high school degree or equivalent. Some of these had some college, but withdrew for reasons of which this study is unaware. Two indicated they had vocational training and more than two subjects were professional tradesworkers without completed postsecondary degrees. It is estimated that 33% of subjects were vocationally trained labor.

Interviews

Once recruited, subjects were scheduled for interviews. I began by using a friend's university office as a fixed interviewing site, but this proved too cumbersome because subjects were unwilling to travel to be interviewed. It became clear that I needed to travel to meet the logistical needs of the interviewees; the same site was rarely used twice for the interviews. Included among the interview sites were community-college cafeterias, public libraries, fire departments, and city park district buildings. Though I tried my best to meet in public places to help ensure my safety, one interviewee refused to meet outside his home, requiring me to set up at his home's dinner table. Once the meeting was arranged, the interview included explanation of informed consent, stimulus transaction, an interview, and a demographic questionnaire.

Stimulus Transaction

The explanation of informed consent is an important formality of human research. Research institutions require that participants be informed of their rights as a participant in a study. Among other things, they are guaranteed anonymity and the right to terminate their involvement whenever they like. Preceding their actual involvement, once they sign a form acknowledging their awareness of these rights and willingness to participate, the interview begins.

Interviews were tailored after Rosenblatt's (1978) transaction research, which characterizes the reading process as a transaction between the reader and the text. She explains, "'Transaction' designates, then, an ongoing process in which the elements or factors are, one might say, aspects of a total situation, each conditioned by the other" (p. 17). To tap the nature of this transaction, as it exists for swing voters' transactions with campaign messages, participants were seated with writing materials near a television and a VCR. They were following instructions verbally:

> Two political advertisements will be shown and you are asked to write down the meanings these spots have to you. You may begin writing as soon as you like, either during or after the spot. After the first advertisement, the tape will be stopped and you will be given as much time as you like to finish describing the advertisement's meaning. When you are through, we will continue with the second advertisement. Afterward, I will ask you some questions and then we will finish with a short questionnaire.

Blank writing materials were provided to the first participant—an interview that proved to be of little value. It was quickly learned that, without prompting the participant with specific questions for the written transaction, almost nothing of any apparent value was written by the participant. Over a period of several interviews, transaction writing materials were developed (Appendix A). Once participants completed the entire transaction with the video stimulus, they continued with the interview.

Several considerations went into choosing the advertisements used as the stimulus (Appendix B). The two advertisements used provided balance between presidential candidates Bush and Gore. The exclusive concern regarding the type of advertisements chosen was about the advertisements' subject matter. Specifically, advertisements dealing with matters deemed most significant in election-2000 exit polls were included. Portrait of America (2000), a division of Rasmussen Research, released a synopsis of "top issue" surveys compiled during Election Day exit polling. Education and social security matters received the highest proportions of "very important" scores on a four-point scale (Portrait of America, 2000). The Bush spot titled "No Changes/No Reductions" addressed social security. The Gore spot addressed college education and is titled "College." Both 30-second spots were borrowed from the University of Oklahoma's Julian P. Kanter Political Communication Archive.

Ethnographic Interviews

Following the completion of the stimulus transaction, informants were engaged in a discussion about the advertisements. All data from the interviews was recorded in two ways. First, each interview was recorded with portable video equipment. Though potentially intrusive, it was the most ideal method for catching the nonverbal components of the interviewees' comments. Second, notes were kept to help document and highlight my thoughts and any notable remarks made by the subjects. It was always the case that the subjects of discussion emerged from attitudes of political advertising but branched into other areas. Interviews lasted about 60 minutes, though this varied because of time availability and interview quality. Though it was the exception, some interviewees just did not provide much insight. Following the interviews, each interviewee was informed of the likelihood of future contact, should the need arise to clarify statements or follow-up for some other purposes. Reflection upon each interview resulted in adjustments in subsequent interviews. Themes began to emerge, and new questions were added to the interview schedule.

After seven interviews, it was clear that very little talk dealt with the advertisements they had been shown. Typically, the conversation moved to address the larger context within which the spots had meaning during the campaign. To prompt discussion of the spots, a book of pictures and text taken from the advertisements was compiled. This was given to interviewees to help stimulate the discussion of the spots. After using this book in a few interviews it proved to be of little value, as subjects made only short critical remarks about the pictures. Some would see pictures of Bush and say, "He's got squinty eyes," while others commented on Gore's posture. Though these types of comments might reflect a cynical attitude or something meaningful about swing voters, it was my opinion that they were the product of excessive prodding, elicited from a communication format they would never have encountered otherwise. Soon after being introduced to the interview process, the book was considered unhelpful and was removed from the process.

Although an initial interview schedule was prepared, it immediately began to evolve following the first interview. Utilizing an approach termed "active interviewing" (Holstein & Gubrium, 1995), interviews were, to some extent, improvised though directed by the project's goal of learning about these voters' approaches to political communication. Despite a few changes, a fairly consistent schedule was used for the last twenty interviews (Appendix A). Eight interview questions constituted the initial interview schedule, and, following a funnel format, more pointed questions were asked later in the interview to avoid introducing topics into the participants' awareness that could influence subsequent answers.

There were two important characteristics of these interviews. Questions asked did not exclusively include those in the appended list. Questions unique to each informant and his/her answers were improvised during the course of each interview. This ability to adapt as the interview progressed allowed me to probe more completely participants' responses as well as their uses of body language. Second, the interview was intended to be a supplement to the written texts produced by participants during the stimulus interaction. As such, interviews followed the researcher's review of participants written comments, resulting in participants' reflections on these comments. This process resulted in questions unique to the written remarks of each respondent.

Demographic Questionnaire

Following the interview each participants was given a questionnaire. This was conducted at the end of the interviewing process to avoid making the viewing situation any more artificial than it already was. Specifically, I wanted to avoid making elements of each subject's socioeconomic status any more salient than it would be in a more natural setting (one wants to be careful to keep his/her respondents from answering questions in light of concerns that wouldn't ordinarily be salient.

METHOD OF ANALYSIS

Geertz (1973) explains that the product of an ethnography should be descriptions in terms of the formula the researcher believes those studied "use to define what happens to them" (p. 15). The method by which the participants' comments were analyzed was consistent with Geertz and his conceptualization of ethnography as an approach to analysis involving "thick description" of social discourse to develop theories about what we believe informants are up to in order to gain access to their "conceptual world" (p. 24).

Although the classical notion of ethnography involves a discreet culture and the immersion of the researcher in it, the present instance is different in that the culture in question is not discreet. Analyzing how swing voters constitute their lifeworld while they are in their element cannot be studied in the traditional sense. There is no physical border to cross to reach the "world" of the swing voter. Because the question at hand pertains to the meanings given to political messages, one can do no better than to give informants an opportunity to interact with political advertisements and to inquire about meaning.

Analysis begins as soon as one is immersed in the data or, as is the case here, as soon as the first interview begins. As seemingly important facets of swing voters' perspectives emerged, hypotheses developed and new questions were added to subsequent interviews. Analysis in a more formal sense was hermeneutic. There are three aspects of philosophical hermeneutics applied in this analysis. First, the notion of the hermeneutic circle is important for explaining the contingent nature of both the comments of informants and the arguments of the researcher. Specifically, interpretation is always done in light of the constantly changing horizon of the interpreter's present as history accrues or sediments "beneath" the present. Thus, observations in this study are only as valid as they are true to the experience of those participating. Years from now, the experience of reading political communication will likely change. Likewise, my own interpretation of this same data will probably change with time. A later edition of this book would likely evidence an altered reading of the responses I received from participants. Again, this does not make the study any more or less valid. Instead, this is the nature of philosophical hermeneutics: the hermeneut must be aware of his/her developing prejudices.

Second, the task of the hermeneut is to identify the prejudices or the prejudgments of the text. Gadamer (1977) writes, "No assertion is possible that cannot be understood as an answer to a question, and assertions can only be understood in this way" (p. 11). To what questions are the participants' responses answers? The answer is not simply "the questions of the researcher." Gadamer's point is more abstract: Their comments reveal an understanding or ground that they accept as solid. The study hopes to reveal on what ontological grounds these individuals make their claims. In this sense, the participants' statements provide a glimpse into the prejudices of those who utter them. In what way a person is predisposed toward a topic or subject is suggested by the manner with which the person speaks of that subject. That a subject is addressed at all betrays a salience in the mind of the person producing the statement. For example, Pat Buchanan's political spot portraying homosexuals reveals his disapproval of the lifestyle. If limiting funds to the National Endowment for the Arts is his proposal, one must ask, "To what question is this proposal an answer?" Perhaps Buchanan's prejudices go beyond a biblically grounded disdain for homosexuality. Perhaps it reflects preoccupation with a Christian tyrannizing image or with a cultural concern with maintaining order and promoting the ideal family that was manifest in television programs throughout the 1950s and early 1960s.

These prejudices do not just happen. As the hermeneutic circle suggests, readers' horizons are always changing, which is another way of saying that their prejudices are altered by experience and history. But one's attitudes can never be abstracted from the context within which they were produced. The attitudes I possess tomorrow will be built on those I have today. Today's attitudes will be sedimented or buried, which is to say they will influence tomorrow's attitudes though I will be unlikely (without reflection) to be made aware of this attitudinal evolution. Essential for understanding philosophical hermeneutics is the idea that if tomorrow's attitudes are built upon today's, then today's are influenced by the attitudes of yesterday.

If the explanation ended here, the reader could be led to believe that the attitudes comprising my horizons are developed during my lifetime. This is only partly true. Certainly my horizons are built, in part, on my experiences of yesterdays and today, but it cannot be ignored that the meaningful place I occupy in time and space is determined for me by the experiences of my culture. It could be said that the sum of these experiences constitute the natural attitude of a culture at a point in history (Husserl, 1954/1970): an unconscious or a preconscious situatedness that enables us to intend or anticipate the world around us. As such, it is argued that horizons are the product of history, and are communicated or shared with subsequent generations through language. Language is the medium through which prejudices, seen as essential for human function in both the cultural and in the natural world (an admittedly contrived distinction), are passed on to a culture's present inhabitants.

This leads to the third aspect of hermeneutics. To understand prejudices, one subjects history to analysis to find the origins of present attitudes. Inherent in this is an investigation of language. Written language, signs, symbols, and architecture represent cultural responses to exigencies faced by the people who produced them. These manifest in our present horizon as traditions. To understand how these language traditions developed, the researcher develops a "historically affected consciousness," that is, an active awareness that the attitudes that give rise to our interpretations are always interpretations contingent upon our constantly accruing history. This is an altogether different way of being in the world; a different consciousness modality.

VALIDITY

Anticipating postmodernism, phenomenology and hermeneutics put forth the argument that upended the Cartesian dualism. Arguing the impossibility of subjectivity and that the truths of "objectivity" were incommensurable, it was maintained that standards for argument were historically contingent cultural products. While scientists pursued objective knowledge by attempting to transcend subjectivity and the biases of their cultural milieu by developing and adopting standardizing language and method, philosophers like Gadamer (1975) focused on the futility of their efforts. Eschewing the dualism between pure objectivity and subjectivity in favor of the thing itself, the philosophical hermeneutic perspective is premised on the rejection of both. Repudiating the myth of the absolute nature of positive science, Gadamer (1975) explains that each individual is always subject to their cultural foreknowledge. For meaning or knowledge to be ascertained, historically situated pre-understandings regarding the nature of what is understood must be adopted. An attempt to shed all prejudices would render the world meaningless and impossible to engage.

As a rejection of the subject-object dichotomy, philosophical hermeneutic's "historically affected consciousness" is a component of a postmodern condition: Gebser (1949) terms it "integral consciousness." Gebser explains that the post-Cartesian mode of engaging phenomena is a state of "diaphaneity" (p. 7). Diaphaneity is a "rendering transparent" of those mentalities or attitudes toward phenomena that constitute the world of those presupposing them. Gebser summarizes this well:

> Contemporary methods employ predominantly dualistic procedures that do not extend beyond simple subject-object relationships; they limit our understanding to what is commensurate with the present Western mentality. Even when the measurements of contemporary methodologies are based primarily on quantitative criteria, they are all vitiated by the problem of the antithesis between "measure" and mass . . . our "method" is not just a "measured" assessment, but above and beyond this an attempt at "diaphany" or a rendering transparent. With its aid, whatever lies "behind" (past) and "ahead of" (future) the current dominant mentality becomes accessible to the new subject-object relationship. (Gebser, 1949, p. 7)

Gebser is arguing that a new "integral" mode of engaging the world has emerged as a response to modernism. Those waring this rupture of the Cartesian dualism acknowledge that meanings associated with things are contingent upon the perspective assumed.

The philosophical hermeneutic perspective problematizes validity because it maintains that truth is contingent upon cultural standards. Despite this, the hermeneut does not avoid producing accurate or truthful statements because of the presumption that one could not fully accomplish the task. Instead, s/he realizes that the production of truth is always in progress and changing in light of developing horizons. Bernstein (1983) explains that "we should always aim at a correct understanding of what 'things themselves' say. But what the 'things themselves' say will be different in light of our changing horizons and the different questions we learn to ask" (p. 139), which is consistent with Geertz' (1973, p. 20) assertion that ethnographic research is a process of submitting one's "better guesses," well aware that "cultural analysis is intrinsically incomplete" (p. 29). In light of this epistemology, Bernstein's (1983) answer to determining validity is by recourse to what a linguistic community considers good judgment, reason, and argument. Truth, he states:

> . . . amounts to what can be argumentatively validated by the community of interpreters who open themselves to what tradition "says to us." This does not mean that there is some transcendental or ahistorical perspective from which we can evaluate competing claims to truth. We judge and evaluate such claims by the standards and practices that have been hammered out in the course of history. (p. 154)

Validity, then, is determined by the community of readers and their standards for sound argument. The following arguments are submitted to you, the reader, for your consideration and your scrutiny. I maintain that these observations are accurate insights and valid explanations for the comments that participants made in the context in which they were uttered. Moreover, these observations are also limited to the extent that the method helped reveal many insights while obscuring observations that the method was ill-fit to access. Nevertheless, by assessing the rigor with which evidence is marshaled, I maintain that the reader will find the analysis and conclusions a valid and heuristic analysis of those individuals studied as well as the larger population.

3

INTERVIEWING SWING VOTERS

OVERVIEW OF ANALYSIS—MODERN VOTING

An overarching theme that runs through the interviews discussed below is one of modernity. The swing voters that participated in this study possessed a modern voting attitude; they approached voting with modern prejudgments. The use of the term *modern* is done with care—it does not mean "contemporary." Instead, this project relies on the notion of modernity as it emerged from the Renaissance. Descartes abstracted humanity from the world, positing a distinction between thinking and extended substance. The premodern attitude could not have presupposed such a separation between humans and the world they inhabited, except as put forth by religion. The world that premodern people encountered or intended was not doubted; it had taken-for-grantedness. Descartes, on the other hand, maintained that the world, as perceived by the individual, was a distorted version of the real—a representation. The world as perceived by mind does its best to approximate the world it encounters, but it could never do so perfectly. Descartes argued that "truth," or ultimate knowledge, could be ascertained through rationality or idealism, avoiding the distractions of the senses. Eschewing the distractions of the world, through proper reasoning, one could tap the "infinite intellect" (Bernstein, 1983).

Descartes' ideas were a catalyst that helped reintroduce Europe to the modern mode of consciousness generally lost during the rise of Christianity and following the demise of Greek influence. His ideas presaged Hume's empiricism, and both shared the pursuit of truth. It was believed by both that truth is knowable through the proper application of method or measurement. Ultimately, these epistemologies influenced governing modalities as increasing numbers of people believed that truth was accessible. Kramer (1997) observes:

> Direction is a choice, and choice is the essence of the democratic cosmos. Moderns perceive, with exclusive validity, an extensive world of spatial (visual) relationships such as linear sequentiality, physical surfaces, and measurement. "Sur-face" means that the world presumably presents an "over" face, common to everyone, which opens the possibility for modern democratic behavior. Each individual can see "the truth" for him- or herself. (p. 103)

The direction of government in a world accessible to everyone through sense and method would no longer be determined by those with divine rights. Resultantly, the divine rights of kings, queens, and property owning white men have been dismantled as suffrage continues to be recognized and expanded in Western societies and others influenced by it.

This project found that swing voters' modern presumptions regarding the determinability of a "right" or "best" candidate compelled them to look for empirical support for their decisions; swing voters are objective voters. This seems on its face to be a good development given our Western modern biases in favor of disassociated and deliberate decision making. The problems argued here stem from the fact that empirical support is generally sought at the expense of subjective experiences. Swing voters do not look to themselves, because their subjectivity would taint their judgment. Instead, they pursue sources external to themselves. As a result, the search for external ground for their voting decisions is coupled with a devaluing of personal needs and concerns. Proceeding from the notion that the knowledge necessary to make a thorough and properly reasoned decision is available to all with the capacity to reason, the individual voter is destined to search for universal and determinable facts existing "out there." Universal truths can't be subjectively produced because these would be contingent truths (dependent upon the vantage point of the voter). Thus, the voter reasons that, "my opinions, feelings, and instincts should not be considered relevant."

Having rejected any reasoning mechanism that could be considered subjective, these voters punt partisan heuristics and other decision-making mechanisms in pursuit of external and verifiable justification for their choices. Frustrating the swing voter is the absence of objectively determined criteria for choosing a candidate. Although this experience should upset the very notion of objectivity for some, swing voters trudge forward propelled by their unexamined and insistent confidence in the determinability of an ideal candidate. Eventually, the voter finds her/himself in the voting booth on election day with nothing other than his/her own attitudes, values, issue preferences, and experiences. Until this point, these have been discounted by them. At the last moment, however, their subjectivity provides these voters with guidance. Despite a voter's better judgment, his/her personal experiences and preferences are utilized to help him/her decide for whom to vote.

Until they vote, however, what have swing voters been doing? The answer is determined by the modern voting paradigm. Like the field analyzed by the social scientist, the campaign or voting milieu should remain uninfluenced by the observer. The role of the scientist is to observe. Likewise, the swing voter plays little or no active role in shaping the field or milieu of the election, except that they are the ones targeted by most campaign messages—a phenomenon observed by Putnam (2001). This "objective" swing voter maintains a distance, simply observing, accruing, and assessing data until the first Tuesday in November. This distance is interpreted by more partisan observers as apathy. My description may initially appear naively benevolent: this impression is dashed, however, by the critique that follows. To the extent that these voters may be deliberate in their approach to politics, they warrant criticism for their general lack of political and social involvement.

Three components of this modern attitude of swing voters are examined in this section. Evidence from the interviews with these voters is provided to evidence these cultural phenomena among the swing voters studied. The observations below are not absolute, and exceptions to the rule do exist. Nevertheless, they are valuable to the extent that they are insightful and revealing. Specifically, this section explains:

1. Why swing voters choose to vote.
2. Why swing voters avoid the biases of party and ideology.
3. Why swing voters strive to be objective (non-subjective).

These three components constitute what is termed by this author the "modern swing voting ethic."

Before I get ahead of myself, it is necessary to explain that this project is not grounded on the modern presumption of the subject/object duality. The hermeneutic approach, grounded in phenomenology, maintains that belief in this duality is a modern prejudgment. Presumption of this subject/object distinction is central to the modern way of living in the world, but it is contingent. It is a product of the consciousness of Western culture unfolding throughout history: cultural adaptations to the exigencies it faced. As the reader proceeds with the analysis, it is important to be aware that any discussion of "subjective" experiences and "objective" knowledge is not intended to reify this distinction. Instead, the project simply attempts to realize

Geertz' (1973) recommendation that the research should provide descriptions in terms that those studied would themselves understand. By not taking this distinction for granted, it is much simpler to conduct analysis, report it in a fashion that is understood, and offer criticism of the attitudes discussed below.

Why Swing Voters Choose to Vote

Most interviews with swing voters revealed their rationale for voting: not the particular vote they cast but the act of voting itself. Swing voters chose to participate in the 2000 presidential election because of a democratic value structure that values participation. The rationale behind this value is abstracted from the purpose of voting, which is to direct government and shape society. This reasoning is circular; these voters believe that it is good to participate in elections because it is bad not to participate. Their remarks make very clear that they voted to perform the meaning laden act of voting for its sake. Although it is suspected that few others, including nonvoters or partisans, would disagree with the inherent value of voting, it is expected that the attitude of the latter group is characterized by the presumption that reasons, political vision, or issue positions should act as a catalyst for voting. A reason should be an antecedent for casting one's vote.

One can find support for these claims in the responses of Subject 2. This is a causasian male community college student in his first year of postsecondary education. He struck me as the type of young adult accused of having little direction, and he joked with me about the irony of his involvement in a study about voting. He displayed many of the characteristics of the young disillusioned political cynic discussed in Hart's (1997) *Seducing America*. Markedly different from Hart's cynic, however, is the fact that this young man cared enough to vote in the first election for which he satisfied the age requirement. He explains that his parents convinced him to vote.

> S2:[1] I didn't really read or listen or think about much of anything till right before the election my parents said, "You know that in a lot of countries people don't have a chance to vote. It's a pity that you have that right and you aren't going to use it just because you think you are uninformed." And I said, "Well, okay, you are right."

If accurately conveyed, the parents' comments are disturbing in their own right—recommending voting without knowledge of the candidates or issues. Nevertheless, this voter was admittedly too apathetic, according to his own standards, to prepare an educated decision. It was on this ground he felt that

---

[1] 'S' is shorthand for *subject* and the number denotes the subject's placement in the interviewing process.

he should not vote. He makes clear in later comments that the perceived *quality* of his decision played a significant role in his initial decision not to participate.

> S2: I don't create the time for myself that I need to really investigate, I don't feel comfortable making a decision unless I know what I'm saying, I don't feel comfortable making an argument unless I know I can back it up, and in voting I feel like I'm making an argument, so.

These are hardly the words of an individual too disenchanted with politics to participate. Instead, this voter views voting as an act that obligates him to responsibly prepare. According to this perspective, if a swing voter chooses not to vote it can reasonably be attributed to an individual sense of inadequacy as much as any general voter disenchantment. In this case, his words reflect a conscientiousness, as he admits that he is ill-prepared. These are the words of a person with standards that he feels he has failed to satisfy. Because this voter teetered between voting for Nader (he disclosed his final decision[2]) and abstaining altogether, he is less representative of the majority of participants who were undecided between the two major party candidates. Nevertheless, nearly all the voters in this study dealt with similar anxieties stemming from a feeling of inadequate knowledge about the issues and the candidates; yet all of them voted seemingly because of their belief that voting is important for the sustenance of a healthy democratic system.

Take as another example the following young voter, Subject 3, an Asian male enrolled at the University of Illinois at Champaign-Urbana. He described a similar voting experience. He explains that he was not prepared to vote, yet he feels that he got swept up in the mentality that voting is inherently good.

> S3: I didn't know the issues. I really wasn't paying attention to the campaign. I didn't watch any of the debates. I didn't know where they stood. You know, I mean the day of the election I just uh went to Web sites to see what, there are a lot of Web sites that show their opinions and their standpoints on most everything.
>
> R: If you didn't feel like you were up to snuff on election day, why did you choose to vote or actually choose to look up that information?
>
> S3: Why did I choose to vote? Prompted by, you know, people on campus down there, everyone wants you to vote. It's more like peer

---

[2]Subjects were never asked to disclose the candidate they supported to avoid any problems associated with the perceptions that I was either prying or that I had any nonacademic or political objectives.

pressure, or you know, a "Rock the Vote" sort of thing. So, I wanted to express my right to vote.

Though awkwardly expressed, from the context of the discussion, the notion of "express[ing] one's right to vote" is easily comprehended. Mass media messages propagate the idea simply that one should vote. MTV's "Rock the Vote" campaign attempts to inform and motivate rookie voters. The Dixie Chicks have recently begun contributing to this effort, stating clearly that they would support "Rock the Vote" without advocating any particular party, though they "will feel free to give our opinion in our personal lives" (Dixie Chicks, 2003). This conception of voting views the act as an end and not a means; the end is manifest as the satisfaction of having performed the act. Thus, voting itself is more of a statement in favor of democracy rather than an endorsement of a candidate or a group of policies. This is made obvious by the language used in the above dialogue; this voter is *expressing* his right rather than *exercising* that right to express a preference. From this vantage point, voting is little more than a celebration of democracy. This individual emerges from the voting booth satisfied that his views have been expressed; no one can accuse him of not expressing his support for democracy.

Subject 8 was a 19-year-old African-American college student at Northern Illinois University. Having failed to learn much about the campaign or the candidates prior to the election, he stated that he believed that he was unlikely to vote. Because of a lack of devotion to the campaign, he found himself undecided because he was sandwiched between the political positions espoused by his parents.

R: . . . why did you ultimately choose the candidate you voted for in the last election?

S8: Um, well me not being necessarily a political person or not necessarily paying attention to the candidates, my mom being a Democrat and my dad being a Republican, uh, they really stressed the issue of going out and voting more or less for their own individual candidates, but going out and voting.

* * *

R: Would you comment on [why you had trouble deciding to vote]?

S8: Um, I guess because I really don't understand everything that goes on, uh, politically, and, I'm not sure what, something was going on. I'm not sure if it was getting close to midterms or finals or something, I really just wasn't focused on it like everybody else was. Uh, but when I guess I did finally decide, ok, uh, I need to go ahead and make a decision or go ahead and vote because my parents were constantly calling me, "come home and vote," "come home and vote."

Most interesting about these comments is that the decision to vote is divorced from the decision regarding for whom one believes s/he should vote. Once he made his voting decision, his job is pretty much complete, because there is little time remaining to brush up on the candidates. Consistent with comments of other subjects, is the absence of a reason *for* voting; a desired end of any kind.

It seemed to me that the active decision about whether to vote was more salient for the aforementioned subjects because of their youth or their scant history of political involvement. In all three cases, these individuals were voting in their first presidential race. As a result, they make more explicit comments about their professed belief in the inherent value of voting. Their comments exhibit an ideology about which these voters are more aware relative to voters with longer histories of participation whose ideologies are more sedimented. Still, this attitude is betrayed by some of the latter group's comments. Several subjects were recruited at firestations in the western and northern suburbs of Chicago. Firestations were particularly valuable for recruiting subjects because of their residents' free time, working-middle-class socioeconomic status, and their typical nondegreed college educated vocational training. I should also mention the affable nature of nearly every person I encountered at these firestations. Subject 27 was a causasian male union fire chief in his late 30s. His following comments reflect his surprise to the response I received when I solicited interviews at the firestation during their lunch period.

S27: I realize the importance of the individual vote, well actually after this last election who knows, but, uh, I still think that the individual vote is important. I was stunned to find out that the guys, when you came in and asked who voted in the last election, 2 out of 3 of us said they didn't. That shocked me, I can't see how any one of voting age can actually, can not. But, uh, it's pretty important, I mean, it's a right.

Evidently, the context of these interviews was shaped by the Florida recount, which explains the acerbic aside about the importance of voting. Central to his statements is the view shared with the college students, that voting is important, ". . . I mean, it's a right!" It is similar to the remarks of the college students, as this swing voter was unclear about who deserved his vote. Though he was a Chicagoland union member, he was not a Democrat, as the stereotype would have it. Likewise, he also had no inclination toward the Republican party. In fact, he never mentioned party until I explicitly asked him what influence party affiliation had on his vote, to which he responded, "None at all." None of his comments revealed a partisan ideology that shaped his vote. As was the case with the others, his ideology primarily valued voting rather than an explicit vision for the nation.

Subject 15 exhibited similar attitudes. This person was a well educated voter; a caucasian male writer in his mid-40s. He holds an MFA and teaches as an adjunct instructor at a large university. As a well educated individual, this person rounds out the individuals cited in this section, because he highlights the fact that the attitudes exhibited by these voters are held by people with varying ages and levels of education. When describing himself, this subject defends his voting history by remarking that he votes. Implicit in this explanation is a negative perception of the failure to vote and, likewise, merit in voting.

> S15: I am a committed voter. I've, uh, I turned 18 when voting was changed to 18, and, uh, I voted in every election. I've never been a, I guess I've always been kind of a more Democratic voter and yet I've never been totally Democratic. I've voted Republican in many elections, in state and local elections. So, I don't think that I'm a well-read voter, but I'm a committed voter and far from apathetic.

Again, party affiliation was not central to this individual's reasoning. According to his comments, party is irrelevant as a decision-making device. In fact, that he even discusses party this way reveals a perspective that views partisanship as a limitation. In his case, there is merit in having voted for candidates of either party. Summing himself up as a voter, he weighs his partisan independence and consistent voting record against his seeming lack of knowledge as a voter who is not well read. He concludes that he is committed. To what? Voting.

To partisans, these voters might seem to be putting the cart before the horse. The swing voter makes up his/her mind to vote before s/he knows for whom to vote. In many cases, these voters decided to enter the voting booth before having made a decision: behavior that must be very puzzling for partisans for whom voting and party are inextricably linked. After all, why vote if there are no political goals the voter intends to achieve? For instance, a Republican might seek a flat tax or an end to abortion, whereas a Democrat might wish to expand national welfare benefits or protect the environment. The partisan's attitude likely produces an approach to the campaign communication environment that is significantly different from that of the swing voter. On the one hand, swing voters may have less time with which to study and formulate a decision than do partisans, though I know of no evidence to support this. On the other hand, it is more likely that the antipartisan attitudes and the resultant decreased concern with issues gives politically relevant information less salience for swing voters. For the swing voter, political information has a limited framework within which it can be made meaningful. It is argued in Chapter 4 that these observations have less to do with a simple lack of philosophy, which is ridiculous considering the broad distribution of swing voters suggests that little difference exists between the way swing voters and partisans are socialized. They have all been socialized around the same ideologies and general cultural influences. More important is a growing devolution of public or community concern. These voters vote to vote; they do not vote to help realize any particular social remedy or vision.

Voting, for voting's sake may not necessarily seem to be a problem. The attitudes behind the "Rock the Vote" campaign are popularly held. In the parlance of punditry, the well-being of U.S. democracy is determined by the percentage of eligible voters who cast a ballot, and relative to other Western democratic nations, the prognosis is typically poor. This attitude in favor of increasing voting volume likely arises from the historic struggle fought to enfranchise marginalized groups. Although all groups are recognized as having an inherent right to vote, it is also argued that democratic nations suffer from "group think" without the benefit of alternative voices. Failure to vote, it is believed, is a sacrifice of one's voice. This attitude, however, presupposes a person has something to say. Although I agree with this idea, I reject the notion inherent in the practice of contemporary voting that much at all is stated solely by voting. The swing voters interviewed in this project walked away from the ballot box with a sense of satisfaction or accomplishment that should be reserved for those who achieve social justice, change, or preservation as a result of their vote. Ignored is the role "voice" plays in governing the issues that actually constitute the election and determine the key players in it—the candidates. In the end, these late deciders may exert little or no influence in the final election outcome. Campbell (2000) explains:

> If late deciding voters remain truly torn between the two candidate (and are committed to voting), we should expect in general that their vote choice amounts to a flip of a coin and thus an even division of their aggregated vote. An even or near even division should raise the vote share of the trailing candidate and reduce the lead of the frontrunner. (p. 47)

If they break evenly at the last minute, then why appeal to them? Perhaps it mitigates their impact. The frontrunner can be comfortable knowing that undecided voters will be unlikely to influence the outcome of the election.

Why Swing Voters Avoid the Biases of Party and Ideology

It was generally found in the discussions with these swing voters that they either explicitly or implicitly viewed any form of bias negatively—a bias against bias. If these voters made their remarks because they genuinely care to divorce themselves from partisan or ideological politics, it reveals an opposition to a group-oriented or ideological approach to politics. On the other hand, if these voters were succumbing to social-desirability bias during the interviews, such that they did not want to seem biased, their remarks still betray their belief that society perceives partisan affiliation and ideological heuristics as harmfully prejudicial. I maintain that these two explanations cannot be separated from one another. One would not believe that avoidance of prejudice was the cultural ideal if it was not influencing, on some level, their own approach to politics. In either event, these outcomes are both enlightening and disturbing as they reflect further the influence of modern bias against bias or a rejection of subjectivity.

Having rejected partisan bias and the use of other ideologies for making sense of politics, how do these swing voters make sense of the information they encounter? How do they subsequently formulate their voting decisions? The best way to make sense of this is to liken modern political decision making to our contemporary approach to professional sports. Take professional football for example. The activity's management is preoccupied with precision, accuracy, and measurement. These concerns emerge from the requirement that competition be fair. Rules are applied equally to all to ensure fairness, conditions are controlled, and referees are impartial spectators. These notions of fairness and equality manifest in the financial management of teams with salary caps and revenue sharing, ensuring that each city has an equal and fair chance of excelling. Having become a spectator's sport itself, politics has increasingly become preoccupied with similar concerns. The state attempts to control any undue influence. The state is barred from influencing politics, campaign finance reform is intended to control the corrupting influence of money, and many voters have become impartial referees—observing performance while withholding judgment. In either case, it is presumed that the outcome will be more accurate if all undue influences are controlled.

These voters are not necessarily employing the language of science, but their discourse is certainly modern. The avoidance of bias, efforts to be fair, and the desire to keep an open mind are evidence of this. For a voter to be fair or impartial rules out the role of advocacy. The reader will see that these voters struggle with their decisions, accumulating as much information as time and interest permit until election day. Most walked into the voting booth with no clear decision in mind. These observations are particularly interesting as they apply to the self-identified partisans. Their talk reveals a fundamentally different approach to being partisan. For them, a gap exists between being partisan and having a cogent understanding of what being partisan means.

Subject 6 was a 60-years-old Asian-American woman. She and her husband were semiretired, working only during the summers and traveling around the United States during the remaining seasons to see their children and grandchildren. She invited me into their cute townhouse in the far north suburbs of Chicago. The townhouse, it seemed, had just sprung forth from a house seed along with the others in the fertile row of identical vinyl sided town homes in a recently developed corn field. The following interview segment strongly reflects the sentiments of many of the interviewees regarding partisanship.

> R: Alright, how would you describe yourself as a voter?
>
> S6: Independent.
>
> R: And explain to me what that means to you.
>
> S6: But, leaning more toward, well, actually I don't. Um, an independent? Well, sometimes I'm moderate and sometimes I'm conservative. Depending on how the issues or whatever.
>
> R: What do you see as tending to make you tilt one way or the other? What kinds of issues or what kind of candidates?
>
> S6: Well, like I don't think that abortion is a platform issue, so I'm not interested in what either candidate has to say about it. I'm conservative in that I believe in term limits, because I think familiarity sort of, you know, breeds contempt. If they are in there too long they are not, I don't know if they have our best interests at heart any more.

At first glance, these comments leave the impression that this voter is the stereotypical independent, typically taken to mean that she is guided more by issues than by party affiliation. In this case *independent* seems to mean what it is *not* as opposed to what it *is*. She can be conservative on an issue, but she does not use the word *Republican*, a word that may entail a uniform ideology for some and an aggregate of shared issue positions for others. One might expect a self-described independently minded woman like this to know the issues and approach voting in a measured and deliberate fashion, voting confidently for the person most qualified on the basis of issue positions. Her following comments reveal that the contrary was true.

> R: Ok, you don't have to tell me who you voted for. I don't care, that's not the point of this question, but why did you ultimately choose the candidate you voted for in the last election?
>
> S6: Um, well I almost never decide until I go into the booth . . .

R: Really?

S6: And usually it's like the lesser of two evils. I was bothered at the very end [of the election] because it seemed like Gore had made some kind of wild statements that weren't exactly true.

R: And that weighed into your decision right at the end?

S6: Yes.

R: Do you think there are a lot of voters like yourself that reason that way and wait?

S6: I would think that there are a lot of people that don't decide until they go into the booth. . . . And then there is people who go in with their paper from the newspaper and just vote exactly that way, and I also had an employer who always voted a straight ticket. And my view was that he was either really lazy or very stupid.

R: Why is that? Why do you perceive somebody who votes a straight ticket as either of those?

S6: That's like saying that um, all Germans are clean. I mean . . .

R: Ok, I follow that.

S6: Or all Italians are good husbands. I mean, that just doesn't make sense.

R: Have you ever gone in to vote for president and had your mind made up well ahead of time?

S6: Um, no not ever really that far ahead.

R: Ok, why do you think you wait so long?

S6: Well, nine times out of ten it is the lesser of two evils. It seems like. Nobody is really that good. . . .

These statements give us a lot to examine. First of all, this voter makes up her mind at the last minute, which does not seem to reflect the behavior of a deliberate and issue-driven independent voter. She is not going to the polls with the hopes of changing, for example, welfare or taxes. Second, she characterizes voters with partisan preferences as "lazy" and "stupid." As additional interviews were conducted, it appeared that these two observations were neither unrelated nor exclusive to this individual. She and voters like her decide late, despite their efforts to avoid "stupidity" by educating themselves about the candidates and their issue positions. Information is accrued, yet the voter is left anesthetized, incapable of rendering a decision because the information is ultimately meaningless. S/he knows what the information means, but it has no valence; it is neither positive nor negative. In any event, their knowledge of issues functions as evidence that they are not "lazy." This woman was operating without a conceptual filter through which she could make judgments about information in the media environment. She may have known a great deal of objective facts about issues discussed by the candidates, but she was ill-equipped to reason about them because she was bracketing the biases necessary to make discriminations.

This attempted withdrawal of bias seems even to apply to their "independent" analysis of issues. Whereas it is unfair to apply partisan predispositions to the assessment of the candidates, it is also seemingly unfair to allow issues to influence judgment. In this case, abortion as an issue is rejected as irrelevant. Other discussions reveal an attitude about being influenced by a single issue, and the perception that this constitutes poor reasoning. Some express the concern that the information one possesses today may be upset by some disclosure or revelation tomorrow. There exists, according to this perspective, multiple and likely valid arguments about issues. Taking a position means "closing one's mind" to that which one does not yet know. Consequently, avoidance of partiality leaves many of these voters incapable of finding solid ground, even when relying solely on issues.

It is not necessarily revelatory that Subject 6 waited until the last minute to decide for whom to vote; after all, late-decidedness is often an identifying characteristic of swing voters. More likely to pique interest is the argument that waiting until the last minute evidences more rational behavior than does the practice of deciding on a candidate well before the election. This extra time allows a person to think and accumulate more information on issues of importance to the voter. It makes little sense to throw one's support behind a candidate only to learn later, for example, that his/her foreign policy intentions are disagreeable or that s/he is proposing an insolvent prescription drug plan, unless your partisan predispositions enable the voter to reason that the positives outweigh the negatives. My argument is counterintuitive; it is in direct contrast to the way late-deciding voters are often perceived, ironically, as lazy and stupid.

Finally, the voting description as a choice between "two evils" should not be overlooked. Subject 6 was recruited at a telemarketing firm during her break. I approached the table where she was seated with several of her co-workers. As the screening questions were asked of all of them, they began speculating aloud about the nature of the study agreeing that the previous election's (2000) selection offered little good from which to choose. This "lesser of two evil" language came up again in her interview as well as in the interviews with others. I suspect that Hart (1997) would call it a "clever" term—the type of term used by cynical nonvoters to provide them with a sense of power or control over an election from which they would otherwise feel impotent. This fails to explain why my subjects used the phrase, considering that they voted and fancy themselves more capable of casting a well-reasoned vote than their partisan counterparts. If it were asked, "To what question is this statement an answer?" it is my suspicion that this "lesser of two evils" rhetoric would perform a face-saving function by helping to avoid the perception that the voter was emotionally involved or irrationally attached to the candidate s/he ultimately chose. It's as if to say, "I voted for Bush, but don't ask me why" or "If he screws up, I never really cared for him anyway!" The comment has as much to do with the perceptions of the candidates as it does with the voter and his/her general (modern) attitude toward voting.

Subject 10 was recommended to me by a professor friend of mine. Knowing what I was studying, he matched me with a nontraditional student whose comments suggested she fit the profile I was pursuing. She satisfied the screening questions, and I sat down with this conscientious, female, Navy veteran in her mid-20s. She describes a very similar attitude about partisan voting.

R: Why did you wait so long to decide for whom to vote?

S10: Well, I, um, I'm not committed to any political party. I don't think that's really a valid way to vote. And, um, I wanted to be as educated as I could on my decision. You know, I wanted to find out as much information as possible. Especially because I was overseas and didn't get to see everything on television, it took me longer to get that information and I didn't get everything offered to me.

R: Had you voted in previous elections?

S10: This [2000 election] was my second; this is the second election that I was old enough to vote for. And I think, I did, I believe I did watch the debates for the first election, but I wasn't as thorough in my, you know, in my research; you know, in my analyzing it. And I wanted to feel like I was making an educated decision, and not just, who looks better.

R: Would you say that in the last election, say in the Dole and Clinton election, that you waited so long for the same reason? How did you go about voting in that election?

S10: Well, um, similarly, but I wasn't as thorough. I think I was younger, and didn't see, I didn't feel that all the issues were as relevant to me. I just didn't, I didn't take it quite as seriously.

R: Did you decide late again [in 1996]?

S10: Yes, but I don't think I waited as long as this time, because I wasn't as thorough and because everything that was on the media in the U.S. was more accessible to me.

R: So the first time you kind of engaged a little late. Would you agree with that? Later in the process. Maybe that's why you made the decision for whom to vote a little late?

S10: Yeah. Yeah. I think, I knew that I wanted; I knew that I wanted to vote, but I hadn't really been paying a lot of attention in the early parts of the campaign. And I, and I, it was almost kind of like procrastinating. I knew; you know I wanted to vote, but I didn't want to go in just guessing. But I had kind of put off the work that I had wanted in order to make an educated decision.

This voter also sees partisan voting as irrational or unreasoned. Instead, she contrasts it with voting as an act for which one must be prepared and educated. In this case, the pursuit of information was the reason behind the late decision. As was the case with subject 6, I tried to explore how she voted without partisan heuristics.

R: Alright, how would you describe yourself as a voter?

S10: Um . . . I don't really know how to explain it, except for uh, because the only time that I've ever noticed it is in regards to certain issues. Like, I'll be having a discussion about one thing and I'll realize, you know, that my view is much more liberal that their's, and in other ways when other people are, have a liberal view, I'm more on the conservative side.

R: Are you just being a devil's advocate?

S10: No, no, no, I'm not, um, I'm not like that at all. Like, I don't argue just to argue. I feel pretty strongly about most things.

R: Would you consider yourself an independent?

S10: Yes, if that means that I don't go with any . . .

R: Have you ever called yourself that? If someone asked, "What party do you belong to?"

S10: I don't think so, probably because I, um, I know that there is you know, because I really don't know exactly what that meant. I didn't know, I didn't want to call myself anything because I didn't really know what that meant.

This individual's confusion about the meaning of "independent" is justified. As noted, its use is better for identifying what one is *not* as opposed to what one *is*. An independent is *not* a partisan, but shares little else in common with other independents. Perhaps this confusion contributed to the demise of Ross Perot's centrist Reform Party which, without an ideology, amounted to little more than a cult of personality. In any event, being an independent does not necessarily offer an alternative to partisan voting. Independence being of little help, subject 10 and others like her indicate that they rely more on issues and evaluations of the candidates' campaign performances.

Subject 24 provided a rich interview. I met this woman at a Bingo game at a Catholic Church in a near western suburb of Chicago. She was a married caucasian woman in her mid-50s who had a daughter about to enter college. We agreed to conduct the interview in a conference room at a public library in Broadview, Illinois. Her comments reflect the decision-making reticence apparent in other swing voters as well as a negative attitude about partisan voting. She also provides a candid glimpse into how she reasons about elections.

R: What caused you to choose the candidate you voted for in the last election?

S24: Um, what caused me to choose? Actually, I was undecided, and when I went in there, I just said, "Well, I heard more about what this guy wants to do, than what this guy wants to do." So, that's who I chose.

This piece of dialogue is very important. Given her use of language, we should be able to predict that this woman is not party-affiliated because she is not reasoning against any type of rubric for determining which candidate is most qualified. When she states "I heard *more* about what this guy wants to do. . . . So that's who I chose," she is measuring which candidate *she* is most qualified to choose. She can best defend her decision in favor of the candidate about whom she knows the most.

R: So, why did you wait so long to decide for whom to vote?

S24: Hmm, because I was unsure. They both had good points and they both had bad points, you know? Um, I don't know, on voting. So, uh, sometimes it's a really hard decision who you want to vote for. Sometimes it's easy. You know, you just go up there and say, "This is who I'm going to vote for, and that's that." You know, I'm sure a lot of people do that; but me, per se, I like to think it over in my mind. Throw it back and forth, you know, who is going to do the best for us.

R: What would have made it easier for you? What do you think would have made your decision easier for you with the last election?

S24: Uh, probably them, um, stating what they are going to do in more laymen's terms, you know, like, "I'm actually going to." Like Bush, he was saying that, you know, he was going to lower the cost of their Medicare and that. But what actually are you going to do? You know, you said you are going to do this, but what actually are you going to do for these people? My mother is retired, you know, and uh, I want to know what actually is going to be out there for her, you know. And, if he really doesn't have time on the commercials or things like that, then they could send out the brochures explaining exactly what they are going to do and you know, in sections. Well, we're going to cut down the cost of say, [if] you are a diabetic. We are going to cut down the cost of say you are [on] diabetic medication and all of that; you know, the needles, your pads, your pills, you know. And my mother is a diabetic, and that would have been real interesting to me, you know, and I would have read that or any number of things, like um, if somebody needs a wheel chair or something and they don't have insurance, you know, they have only got the Medicare, sometimes it doesn't pay for everything, you know. Well, if they say, "Well, you only. If Medicare doesn't pay for it, then you don't have too. You get it anyways." That would have been interesting to me too, you know, to find out exactly what he is talking about. I think that if they are going to make promises then they should send out a thing saying exactly what promises they are actually going to do, and what's effecting that, you know.

R: Is it safe to say that when you watch an advertisement you are not looking at it from a Democratic or a Republican perspective, but instead the guiding principal is to determine which candidate is going to help you most.

S24: Right. Yeah. I don't look at it as a Democrat or a Republican. I look at it as which one is going to do the best for the country and for the people. That's the way I look at it.

One might suspect that without party the voter would need to rely on an alternative vision, either general or specific, for positions on particular issues. In this interview, the respondent indicates a strong interest in Medicare and Medicaid. She expressed concern for her mother, and apologized off-camera for physical challenges of her own, as she exhibited tremor-like symptoms in her hands. I looked for her to unpack the phrase "best for the country." She responded, "I think that, you know, it just seems that like every year everything is going up higher and higher and our paychecks are not getting up that high. That's what I'm saying." Initially, her expressed concern about the country's best interest suggests that her vote is guided by some general community concern, but her explanation was more immediate and self-centered. With little more than this to go on, there is little surprise that she cast her vote for the candidate she knew more *about*, a quantitatively determined vote—thoroughly modern.

The bias against bias appears to influence how swing voters approach the value of interpersonal communication in determining their votes as well. Subject 9 was a 20-year-old female, African-American student who responded to a classified advertisement I'd placed. She explained that she was careful about messages originating with campaigns as well as with her campus peers.

R: Why do you think you waited so long to choose a candidate?

S9: Um, I was kind of confused at first.

R: About what?

S9: Just about, because if you just hear things about one candidate, it is like, it could just be hearsay or [unintelligible]. I think I kind of wanted to see for myself, or kind of listen up for who was about what.

R: Do you think you have a predisposition toward either party, or do you keep an open mind?

S9: Uh, pretty much I keep an open mind; I mean, it's kind of hard, when I hear other people talk about it.

R: Really? What is hard?

S9: Like if someone keeps saying this person is for that, and he's not, he's this or that you know, and so you are like, "hmmm?" So I think I kept pretty much an open mind and I just kind of listen for myself, because, you know, there are a lot of people on campus talking about it, you know what I mean?

R: Well I am interested in that. What are they talking about . . . Bush?

S9: There were like people from both parties came to talk, so, we got to hear both sides a little bit. I think, the one I voted for appealed to me more.

R: When you talk about it being difficult because people are talking about it, do you mean that people that came to campus or do mean your peers?

S9: No, it is like peers and, you know, people.

Again, anxiety over fairness is apparent. The woman explains that she has to keep "an open mind." This person exhibits concern that information received through other people, regardless of who they are, can be tainted. She has to "see for herself"—seeing is believing. Although she admits she probably should have known more about the candidates, she believes that her approach to voting is ultimately more "fair" than the partisan alternatives.

R: How do you describe yourself as a voter? When it comes to formulating your decision and that?

S9: Like, probably not the best voter but like I only voted one other time before this you know; so, I think that, like that one, I kind of knew, but I didn't really know; so when there is, really, I'm not as much to the point where I should know like a lot of people are. But, I think I keep an open mind.

R: What is the best voter?

S9: The best voter would be kind of research on both candidates, you know; find out, you know what I mean they, kind of, if you are really into it, you know, you find out what each one is about yourself and you are not really leaning towards what other people are saying

R: Then what do you think about people who pretty much have their minds made up as soon as the conventions are done? It doesn't seem to be the best voter that already has his mind made up?

S9: I don't think it is really fair; because, a lot of times they are going on what other people say, too, and it is like: you got to vote for what you want and what they can do for you. If you are going on someone else, it is not going to help at all, really.

She is guided with fairness and a dose of self-interest; neither evidence the role of a more general social concern in the final formulation of her vote. Strangely, her efforts to be fair undercut one of the most important tools she has to help make her decision—public engagement or deliberation. She dismisses the comments of others as hearsay because of concerns of validity and bias. However, without these interactions, the values with which she assesses candidates cannot be challenged, strengthened, or revised.

R: Um, now I don't ask the next question because I care who you voted for and you don't have to tell me, but ultimately why did you choose the candidate in the last election that you chose?

S9: Um, I just looked at more of what they were focusing on; I mean, and, just, I guess, a lot of it had to do with things that I had heard about both candidates, like things they were saying, stuff about other people or other candidates, so, like I didn't know a whole lot about either of them, but, from what I knew most about, I felt more comfortable with the one I chose.

Her talk reflects a presumption that she has to vote. Like someone on a car lot who needs something with which to get to work tomorrow, a choice *must* be made today. Similarly, that she will vote is presupposed. The end is the vote. From what she "knew most about," presumably an issue, she decided that she was "comfortable" with her decision. Besides this, no criteria were mentioned.

A theme of fairness runs throughout the comments of the following individual. Subject 13 was a 60-year-old woman from the far western suburbs of Chicago. She disclosed that she had two married adult children and grandchildren. At this stage of her life she maintains her home and helps her husband manage several rental properties. She is a terrific example of a swing voter, as she indicates that though she supported Gore in the 2000 election, she voted for Dole in 1996 and Bush in 1992. She explains that she has no partisan allegiances and tries to be objective when assessing the candidates.

R: What do you think about people that have got their minds made up about a month before or two months beforehand?

S13: Well, they either really, really like that person, or some other reason. You know, that their mind is closed to not paying, you know, giving the other one a chance, or taking a look at them both. I don't think you can make up your mind completely. I think you need an open mind on both people, and then make a decision. But usually, I don't wait this long, like I did this time, but like I said I didn't like either one. I felt like I didn't have a choice.

R: So would you say that someone who goes and blindly votes a straight ticket is a good voter?

S13: No. No, but when you go out and you declare yourself Democrat or Republican, I don't feel like I want to do that, one way or the other. That's why I don't go out in the primary.

R: What else is there besides just voting regularly that makes a person a good voter?

S13: Well, I think a person needs to read, you know, about the candidates which, you know, we get delivered to the house here on everybody that's running, and I do basically read the pamphlets, you know; and I tried to watch some of the debates. And I watch a lot of news, if it has to do with politics. Or if it, you know—I can't say that I'm a sharp person as far as politics, because I'm not—because I'm not really into politics. But when it comes to the president or governor, something like that, I take interest.

* * *

R: Why did you wait so long to decide who to vote for?

S13: Because I was unsure. I didn't like either one. Bush I don't like because he came from Texas and I'm against the death penalty, which they have a lot, you know; which is done a lot in Texas. Gore, I didn't particularly like him. Maybe it had to do with Clinton, I don't know. I shouldn't let Clinton rub off on Gore.

R: How do you prepare to vote?—other than, you mentioned that you read the mailers and watching the debates—what else would you say you do as you work your way up to Election Day, to make up your mind.

S13: Well I just try to read the pamphlets that come in. You know, watch the TV, the news, and I watched the parts of the debates. I didn't watch them all.

R: What about past elections? Past presidential elections?

S13: I voted in them all.

R: Have you been split though, just, similar to the way you were in this election?

S13: No, I don't think so. I'm trying to think who ran, uh,

R: Dole?

S13: No, I didn't vote for Clinton, that's for sure. And when Clinton ran the first time, I voted for Bush. So that didn't have any bearing on me not voting for his son, because I did vote for him [the older Bush]. No, I just take a look at the individuals, you know, and try to learn about their backgrounds and everything, you know.

These comments are terrific support for Wattenberg's (1991) thesis that voters base their judgments on incumbent performance. Though not stated explicitly, one can find in her talk the presumption that her job is to size up the relative characters of the candidates. Character impressions were what subjects most often volunteered. Though I eventually asked each subject about issue preferences, they rarely mentioned much. Subject 13 kept her mind open; she did not "like either one." Biasing one's self toward one candidate, according to this individual, denies the opponent the chance to which he should be entitled.

The following two cases demonstrate that the previous observations may also apply to individuals *with* partisan affiliations. More specifically, these individuals came from very partisan households and had strong Democratic group affiliations. Nevertheless, both reasoned that the influences of these affiliations were improper. Subject 16 was an African-American woman from the near southern Chicago suburb, Markham, Illinois. She was interning somewhere in the city when she responded to a classified advertisement I placed in the *Chicago Reader*. She explained to me that her whole family voted for Democrats and that she did not think that this was right—Bush deserved a chance.

R: Now, you told me that you made up your mind to vote in the last couple of days.

S16: Yeah, because I was *listening*. I was like, ok, yeah. I didn't really like Bush, but I didn't want to just not vote for him just because I didn't like, *like* him. I guess I'm a Democrat, I don't know; whoever, I listen to the issues.

R: That's fair. Is this the first presidential election that you have voted in?

S16: Yeah, I'm 21. Yeah.

R: If you consider yourself to be a Democrat, why did you even . . . What does it mean to you that you were giving Bush a chance, or you wanted to hear what Bush had to say?

S16: Because, I'm allowed to *choose* . . . I mean, they are people, and people make mistakes. So, I don't want to say, "Ok, I'm a Democrat, so I'm just going to stay Democratic." Because, you know, you could be a Democrat, but you could be saying totally something totally wrong which is probably not too far off, because like the Democrats are like mostly the same, but you could have a different vision than like I have, so, I have to like listen to the issues and what you have to say and what's like behind, try to get a look at like what's behind, try to get behind your thinking before I'll say, "Cool, I'm going to vote for you just because."

* * *

R: How do you describe yourself as a voter?

S16: Is that like the liberal/conservative thing?

R: No, when it comes to choosing who it is you want to vote for and uh . . .

S16: I choose, I guess, somebody that is most like my morals and values, who like, wants the same that things that I would want. Or like who is talking about positive things like education or, I guess, Medicaid is no big deal because my grandmother, like all the old people in my family, have insurance. If they wanted to go to the doctor they could go. But, I guess if I had a grandmother who was sick or elderly, I mean, it would probably be a bigger issue, but for me, that education thing—he was talking more along the lines of things that would help me. But as I get older I'll probably change and modify.

R: Why did you choose the candidate that you chose?

S16: Damn. I *like* Clinton. I thought Clinton was a cool person. I wanted to change the two-term thing and bring him back. But I liked the way Clinton ran his camp, per se, his camp when he was there, and I knew Gore was a part of that. I knew that when Clinton was in office, he changed a lot of stuff. You didn't really hear a lot about Gore when he [Clinton] was president, but you could see that they were mostly coinciding at the same time, so, uh, I liked Gore.

R: When did you start paying attention?

S16: Well, I meant to watch the debates and stuff, but I didn't get a chance. So, maybe like that last week, you know; the last week right before the election they start throwing out a lot of stuff, um, like the debates overall, or on the news they say like, "Remember this debate during the Fall" or whatever they said. So, I just start watching the news like a week before; or like Nightline, like a week before.

R: Okay, um, why do you think you waited so long to engage in the election and to decide who you wanted to support?

S16: I had like *no* time. No time, as a student, if you have to like write a paper. It is like, really nice to like sit down and watch TV; I would rather sit down and watch a complete, entire show during the week, so, and usually that is like on Thursday, and I have something. Or, we'll just talk about it in a class of mine, in class or something, some class I had; and we were talking about it, so I was just, I didn't have time. I really didn't have to sit down and research and put, oh, "He went to Harvard. He was an A student." So, I had like no time to really get to know the candidate.

R: If that is the way you describe how you ended up voting, what would the ideal, how would the ideal voter in your mind prepare to vote?

S16: He would watch the debates. Know the candidate, because he can inevitably run the country and can change a lot of stuff, but there are always checks and balances, but he's the president. So, I think you should watch the debates, know what's important to you, not just meditate on "What's important to me now?" but like, education, child care credits, affirmative action, stuff like that is *important* to me, so I would watch the debates. I would look at the whole scope, but the things that I really want that are important to me, I would home in on each candidate to see where both of them stood.

R: Now, it's interesting to me that you wanted to - you engaged late, say a week before the election - you gave Bush a chance, you *wanted* to hear them out. Um, what kind of a chance do you think Bush had of getting your vote?

S16: Like 30%.

R: 30%?

S16: Yeah.

R: Why? Was there anything in his favor that you liked?

S16: I'm trying to think what I liked about him, because now every time he's on TV I'm just like, "ick, ick, ick." He was *such* a phony. I don't know, let me think, what did I like about him? I liked that he was kind of like a family man, because he was like family-oriented. Well, he was like on TV, but I guess if you are going to be a political figure, you *have* to be a family man. But you could tell that he was genuinely genuine with his family. That's why I was like so, he has to have some like Clinton in him *somewhere*. Right. So, I use the 80/20 rule. If you have a 20% chance, no, I mean an 80% chance, it could work. So, he had thirty, so he was tipsy, but Gore, Gore got it, my vote.

Unlike most of the other voters included here, she was guided by traditionally Democratic issues, yet she still withheld her decision in order to be fair because she is "allowed to choose." Regarding her comments, the researcher has to give the subject the benefit of the doubt when she states that Bush had a 30% chance of getting her vote. Even if she considers herself partisan, the very meaning of *partisan* has fundamentally changed if voters are keeping "open minds" in order to be fair or objective. The very idea of being partisan precludes having a completely open mind; a partisan person is inherently biased, and elections are opportunities to make manifest the values and wishes of the party, many of which she expressed during this exchange.

Subject 25 was a caucasian grade school teacher in the near southern suburbs of Chicago. She grew up in Chicago, was an active member of the National Education Association, and states that she has always been a Democrat and yet she was undecided up to the moment she entered the voting booth. Despite all of her affiliations, her desire to be fair and open-minded tempered her history of partisanship. I also suspect that she may not have been capable of articulating a clear description of a Democratic philosophy, which may have less to do with her and more to do with the lack of ideological cogency on the part of the party. In any event, had her partisan affiliation had a rich meaning for her, it is unlikely that she would have uttered the following comments.

R: Okay, ultimately I'm interested in learning why you chose the candidate you chose. You don't have to disclose who you voted for because that doesn't help me in any way, but if it comes out and you don't care, that's fine, also. But, why did you choose the candidate you chose?

S25: The reason why I chose the candidate I chose again, is I was raised a Democrat. I mean, you never went outside the Democrat. I mean, both of my parents are gone now so I kind of just think I'm suppose to carry that over, as dumb as that may seem. And then, being in education, I mean, the union pushes. You know, so that bottom line when you are going to regist[ister], going to vote, I mean, you've got that NEA card and it's kind of like, I mean, it's probably not very smart to say, but that's what geared me toward it.

R: So, if you have all these influences pushing you to vote Democratic, why did it take so long to decide who to vote for?

S25: I guess because I wasn't really keeping up on every, you know; I wasn't watching the news and listening to all the debates and everything and I really wasn't sure. I heard really good things about Bush, you know: the little things I was seeing on the commercials and everything; and I like, this video that I watched today, you know, I was impressed with it. Um, Gore, you know, he's a Democrat: I'm supposed to go that. So it was like a *toss*. I mean, it was almost like if I didn't, I felt like I was going against what I was raised to be, you know; it's probably embarrassing to even say that, but, you know, I felt a certain loyalty, I think.

R: Would it be safe to say that you were getting these messages to vote Democrat, but you didn't feel like you had enough information or you started real late in the election paying attention, and made up your mind at the last minute. Not because it was so much a toss up but because you felt it was fair to hear both sides out.

S25: Right and, believe it or not, there is a *lot* of pressure out there when it comes time to vote. I mean, I remember growing up and I knew that my parents were Democrats. But when your friends came over, nobody ever talks about it. But now, people will just come right out and tell you, "You can't vote this way. You can't vote that way." You know, um, you know it's funny because when my husband even found out, he goes, "Well, what are you going to do?" And I said, "Well, I'm a Democrat, I don't know what to do." And then at the last minute he goes, "I'm going to vote just to outdo your vote." You know, it gets to that kind of a, you know. Um, so, it was a bit confusing, but the bottom, when it came down to it, it was like that loyalty, it just. . . . But it does make me want to, next time around, I think I'm going to pay more attention, because I don't think it's, it's as important anymore as being strict, you know, party per se.

* * *

R: When do you think you started paying attention?

S25: I think as it got closer in; probably, I mean, *actually* when I knew that I was going to *have* to make a decision. Not until the last month, maybe.

R: That's when you started watching and...

S25: Yes.

R: How do you prepare to vote?

S25: Um, how do I prepare to vote? I just try to get—I don't have the patience really to sit and watch all of the debates—so I just try to get, just from like, the next day in the newspaper or something, just the main points, you know. Even like with this, with Gore, with what took me back; I know Gore was for education, and we know education, and based on what I heard, it did bother me that he isolated it to one class, kind of.

R: Why aren't you watching the Bush ad as a Democrat and beating it up along the way, or being a little more cynical about it?

S25: I think—because when I look at ads I think there's, on both parts, not just the Republican or the Democrat, I mean—I think they do *promise* a lot. I'm just hoping that there would be at least somewhat of what they are saying is *true*. And, I mean that would go for *both* sides. And, I think that I have a real big concern for the elderly and I think that it's because of the people in my life and I see how scary it is for them. Even if what he said, even only came through in half of what he said, I think it's better than nothing, you know what I mean? Where it's at right now? So, I, it just didn't, I'm not a Republican *hater*. You know what I mean? And some people are black and white; actually, my brother-he asked me right out who I was voting for! And he lives in Florida, so when all that stuff was happening in Florida, you know, it was something! He was yelling at me because of who I was voting for. You know, I'm not a hater of the party, I'm not; it's more of that loyalty kind of issue and a lot of times, just not paying any attention: it's ignorance. You know, I don't listen, or I didn't listen, and I don't know all of the issues that they're talking about, so I wouldn't think it would be fair, you know?

The last few comments are characteristic of most of the interviews. She does not possess a cynical attitude towards the advertisements. Like most others she was a bit dismissive, most likely, for the reasons mentioned above—a distrust that everything that is said is not precisely accurate. Nevertheless, these perceived exaggerations or inaccuracies are viewed by these voters as part of the nature of the presidential campaign, and looked past in order to learn the general views of the candidates. This is relevant to the following section because this sense of fairness works two ways. First, these voters withhold judgment of campaign information so often dismissed by others as rhetoric. Second, these voters maintain a critical eye with respect to seemingly more objective sources of information (e.g., news). They are impartial toward both. Though she employs cynical talk, she is not cynical. Cynical talk should be recognized as part of political talk—a discursive defense against the perception that one is being huckstered. Moving beyond that talk, however, we find a woman under pressure to learn about and know the candidates. She wants to know. She is not cynical.

Interestingly, she describes herself as "not a Republican hater." This statement would be unnecessary if it was believed that being partisan presupposed acceptance of and respect for opposing views on political matters: one need only watch CNN's Crossfire, Fox News, or the Clinton vs. Lazzio senatorial debate to be certain of this. The notion of political coexistence barely hangs on. Limbaugh tells his audience, "We're winning folks!" and Gingrich says "We've only landed on the beaches." Increasingly, parties are viewed as fighting one another, struggling to *vanquish* their foes rather than co-contra-conspirators in the quality functioning of the democratic process. This attitude about parties is discussed in the following chapters.

In the case of the latter subject, she "is" a Democrat, as if to say it is genetic code inherited from her parents. She is born into a fight, but the struggles no longer have the significance they once held for her parents. For instance, by blood I am Irish. However, being three generations removed from the nation of Ireland, I am relatively ignorant of the history behind its resentments and religious struggles; my uncle, brother, or mother never had trouble worshipping as a Catholic. With thousands of miles guaranteeing my safety, the nuances of the conflict between the Catholics and Protestants elude me. Similar to political parties, political fighting, for many, becomes an immutable way of life. Others drop out or find different ways to make meaning of it all, including ignoring politics altogether. The Democratic Party is not a group this respondent ever consciously joined and does not know the "creed" (though she carries relevant cards). This seems evident when she states that she "heard good things about Bush." That she entertains Bush at all suggests her party ties are loose. Her statement reveals that it came as a surprise to her that there were good things to be said about a non-Democratic candidate. This presupposes that the Republican candidate typically has little good to be said about him, but in this case, she has heard the opposite. For this reason, Bush is considered an option by this voter; so long as the Republican cannot be simply dismissed as bad, he has earned a chance to be considered—until the last minute. *This is only fair.*

Why Are Swing Voters Objective?

Several years ago, while teaching public speaking at a college in northern Illinois, I was explaining the role of persuasion in the public deliberation of ideas—a process necessary to shape society. During the lecture, I explained that if students wanted to reduce federal regulations they could fight to repeal regulations of their choice. Likewise, if they wanted to regulate land by socializing all of it and distributing it equally, they could do that as well. One student raised his hand and rather confidently stated that we couldn't do the latter because that constituted communism. When I said, "So what?" he shrugged and looked puzzled both by the fact that I questioned the logic of his statement as well as by my own logic. I continued to explain that if a majority of society wanted to support such a change, they could make it so. This student's attitude is indicative of one held by many: a general acceptance of society's structure as natural, non-negotiable.

The objective voter approaches politics in a similarly passive way. Swing voters are objective voters: political bystanders governed by a sense of fairness. By watching, reading, and accruing information, they play their part in the political spectacle while advocates (campaign practitioners) perform their own part. This is an artificial and potentially harmful distinction as the only people with agency in this scenario are the advocates; they shape the debate while the voters listen. Participation in the debate is precluded by the passive role of the objective voter. From this perspective, it seems that the debate and the issues defining it simply emerge from the ether. Just like my students' views on society, issues arise naturally and are non-negotiable.

One of the debates among observers of U.S. politics pertains to the health of our democracy. Some scholars and pundits imply that the strength of a democracy can be determined by measuring active partisanship.³ Without using or valuing party preference as a heuristic device for decision-making swing voters are constrained further because their general efforts to be impartial cause them to devalue their own interests.

What remains for the objective voter as s/he tries to formulate a decision? They are fixated on information, and discuss it in terms of both quantity and quality. Presuming a "right" or "best" candidate is determinable, the objective voter highly values information pertaining to the candidates and issues. Objectively determining the "right" candidate is an impossible and ultimately frustrating task for the swing voter for several reasons. First, the voters have an inadequate framework with which to make meaning of information. No matter how much data they accrue, their strictly imposed freedom from prejudice predisposes them to dismissing information that is seemingly too compelling. In fact, interviewees rarely made a negative comment about one candidate without balancing it out with a negative comment about the other in order to demonstrate their impartiality. They seemed determined not to make a decision. Second, because of the perceived and actual limits on available time, as experienced by these voters (as well as many other members of U.S. culture), they never felt like they could get enough information. Competing with all of the other demands of the day, concerns about catching up on politics took a back seat. Although amassing "enough information" is a Sisyphean task, these voters didn't seem to see it this way. That they never get enough information is perceived as a function of the media, campaign, or their own limitations of time or interest (I don't think these two can be separated). The final root of swing-voter frustration stems from the simple faith in or presumption of a determinable right candidate. At least Sisyphus could see the top of his hill. Objective voters, on the other hand, push indefinitely. With no ideological trajectory, they simply accrue information and run out the clock: deciding at the last minute because no time remains.

Many subjects were asked how they imagined the ideal voter prepares to vote. Their responses reveal a shared ideal about how one should go about voting. It is an ideal, I'm afraid, even partisans fail to meet. Subject 3 shared such a perspective. Absorbed in his studies at school, he found little time to follow the election.

R: What role do you think political ads played for you in the last election?

---

³Several studies have measured the level of partisan voting in presidential elections (e.g., Campbell, 2000). It is implied that these voters are more enthused and less apathetic about participation. While some have lamented the overall decline in voting, Campbell's argument suggests U.S. politics is well inasmuch as "partisanship in the electorate is pervasive and has not changed much in the aggregate from one election to the next" (p. 33).

S3: Um, none at all, I didn't really see that much. To be honest with you, I really didn't see too much. I don't recall any. I don't remember seeing any ads. So, they didn't play any role at all.

R: Why aren't you encountering these ads?

S3: I don't know. I just don't watch TV at the right time. I don't know. I saw a lot of local district ads. Representative ads but I didn't see that many presidential ones.

R: When you say you characterize yourself as unknowledgeable, does that mean . . . I mean, I can take a lot from that. I can say that you see yourself as not up on current events, or don't care about events, or that you are too busy with your studies . . .

S3: Yeah, well, relating back to the last election, I just didn't really take the time to sit down and watch debates, watch CNN, CNBC; I just didn't sit down read the paper, watch TV or anything, you know, I didn't, you know; it's not that I didn't care. I *do* care to a certain degree. But I just didn't take the time to find the facts or find their standpoints.

R: If that's not the knowledgeable voter then what, how would you describe the ideal voter?

S3: The ideal voter I think, first of all he has a mindset of, you know, he's either a Democrat or a Republican. You know me, I don't know what I am; you know, um, he knows the issues, he knows what it means to be a Republican; I don't even know what it means to be a Republican. You know, typically down the line, Republicans have this sort of view on things; Democrats have this. At least that's what I feel sometimes. A typical voter knows this. He knows the facts, he knows history of the candidate, he knows where he's been, what he's done, his policy on this, his policy on that, future policies if elected. He knows all these things. I think that would be the ideal knowledgeable voter.

It's noted earlier that this individual decided to vote because of the sense of obligation instilled in him by others—the "Rock the Vote" sort of thing. Prior to this decision, he was disengaged, failing to live up to the standards he felt voters should meet. These standards are pretty extensive, and they are echoed by a number of other subjects.

Subject 17 was a male in his mid-20s. He was a carpenter attending classes at a union apprentice school near Chicago. This person was genuinely split between the candidates because he agreed with both of them. Gore supported his union while Bush's ideas were more consonant with his Christian beliefs.

R: So, what did you think of Gore as a candidate back then?

S17: From those advertisements or in general?

R: From that advertisement or other advertisements you saw, and in general.

S17: I was influenced a lot by Gore because of the union and stuff like that. But, surprisingly, I didn't even vote for Gore. I voted for Bush, but uh, Gore was definitely pushed in people's faces a lot. A lot less or a lot more than Bush was, through the advertising aspect of it.

R: Well, you said you liked Bush. What did you like about him?

S17: Just rumors, I guess, from people on the street. Gore, I didn't really like because of things he believed in that were like not morally correct for me, like the prolife or abortion aspect of that. And a couple of others things in his speeches that I just didn't really like. I found out at the last minute what I didn't really like about him, and I thought I was going to vote for him the whole time, and then at the last minute, no.

R: Um, ultimately why did you choose the candidate you voted for? How would you wrap that up?

S17: I voted for Bush because of my morals. Because he didn't believe in a lot of things I believed in, but Gore believed in a lot of things I didn't believe in. Like, Gore made it aware that he believed in certain things that I didn't like, and Bush never, he had a no comment on a couple things, and said he did not agree with Gore for the other reasons, so he really didn't say, he really didn't say anything bad, but Gore went out and said a couple of things that I did not like.

R: Then why did you wait so long to decide who to vote for?

S17: I don't know. I was choosing between my morals and my workplace basically. One's going to help me as a person and another's going to help me spiritually or morally or whatever you want to say about it.

R: Would you consider yourself pretty religious?

S17: No. I go to church every Sunday but that's about it.

*　*　*

R: How would you describe yourself as a voter?

S17: Unaware, because I was very unaware of a lot of things that were going on during the whole election.

R: What, how does the aware voter behave? What sets him or her apart from how you go about voting?

S17: Probably did a lot more, people did a lot more research than I did. Probably watched a lot more speeches than I did, and probably watched a lot more speeches than I did, and probably read a lot more of the newspaper about the two candidate than I did. And, uh, maybe had better beliefs than I did?

All of this dialogue is included because it documents some of the cross-pressures dealt with by this respondent as he formulated his voting decision; it addressed his views on political information in general. As such, it evidences an obvious struggle between workplace pressures and personal religious beliefs. Whereas others discussed abortion as an issue, this was the only individual to raise the topic of religion as a guiding ideology. Though this voter is an exception because his vote is guided by an ideology, his opinions illustrate well the swing voters' approach to information. The ideal voter, in his opinion, does more research, reads newspapers, and watches speeches.

Anxieties about quantity of information are coupled with concerns about quality. In fact, each subject was asked his/her opinions about the advertisements watched and nearly each of them was capable of scrutinizing the methods with which the ads were produced. Among many other things, they know that the spots are meticulously produced, that Bush's neckties are chosen for him while Gore's earth tones are custom picked, and the people depicted in the ads are carefully selected to represent key constituencies, and to convey a valuing of diversity. These comments were volunteered without prompting and they were expressed without the expected know-it-all tone. Instead, they adopted a *voice of resignation* acknowledging that these practices were *the craft of politics*. They understand this, and it does not cause them to withdraw. They are less cynical than they are cautious, a warranted attitude considering that methods of campaigning have increasingly become the focus of campaigns and policy. A similar skepticism was directed towards news sources, characterized by awareness that writers always have a slant, angle, and vantage point from which they report the events they witness.

This is an important area of the analysis because it seems to relate directly to Hart's (1999) arguments that voters have become too cynical, all too willing to criticize the politicians and information that occupy the public sphere. Still, the words of these voters are not as cynical or clever as Hart would have it. Their criticism seems balanced, considered, and reasonable; there is little evidence of a knee-jerk skepticism. Subject 17 volunteered the following concern:

> S17: I don't know if they are made with a lot of bullshit or if they are actual truths or if they are just saying what people want to hear. I don't know.
>
> R: So you wouldn't go so far as to say you know for sure it's bullshit, but you wonder sometimes.
>
> S17: Yeah, I wonder if it's bullshit.

Is this a flippant dismissal of politicians' talk? I probed him and asked about the source of his skepticism.

> S17: It seemed like they were trying to, I mean, it seemed that they couldn't do everything they were going to say they were going to do. But like, because if they're going to do it, how come the last person didn't do it? Or, if it shouldn't even need to be fixed. If there is a president today, why should that stuff even need to be fixed? They should be doing it as they go along, you know?

This seems like healthy skepticism. He struggled deciding between two candidates because of different policy positions with which he agreed; he was clearly engaged enough to vote and reason about the candidates and their positions. This is tempered with a healthy dose of uncertainty about the ability and sincerity of candidates and the feasibility of their ideas.

While at sea, subject 7 was forced to rely more on peers than did other participants. Information was a little scarcer so she had to take advantage of what she could access. Nevertheless, she still expressed care about the angles from which information was produced, whether by campaigns or the "more objective" news sources.

> R: Okay, how do you describe yourself as a voter? Answer that any way it makes sense to you.
>
> S7: How do I describe myself as a voter?
>
> R: Yes.

S7: Mature. Because I at 20 didn't care either way. And now I'm getting older and I realize that social security effects me, education effects me. I'm going to be a teacher, and that effects me. That education . . .

R: So how does a mature voter prepare to decide how to vote in an election?

S7: Conversations with peers, a lot in the newspapers and the media. It's the only way that I can, I can get to it. You can go on Web sites now, because they have online access to a lot of stuff. I guess you always have to remember that they're biased towards what they want you to read. If it's in a newspaper, you have to remember that that's coming from that writer's perspective. So, I take what I'm reading and try to believe half of it, and realize that it's also coming from [unintelligible].

R: So, you are being kind of critical then about the sources that you are using.

S7: Right, I try to get a lot of people; I try to talk to a lot of people. Because I am not very political; I don't, I do try to pay attention to what's going on around me as far as politics, but I couldn't, there are some people that are way, probably yourself being one of the people that really follow politics, but I don't have a clue about a lot of this stuff. So, you know my mom is a strict Democrat, and she will not vote any other way no matter what. And to me that makes no sense. I can't say that I'm that way, not that I feel that I should be, but . . .

R: What do you feel about people like that? Be nice to your mother, but what do you feel about people in general that are very staunch either Republican or liberal. They know exactly who they are going to vote for the second the convention is done.

S7: Well, I guess in some aspects I wish that I would have that conviction. But I don't think that I could have that faith in those people- it's *politics*. They're not always going to be honest. They're going to be, they're going to say what you want them to say and, hopefully, from what I understand, if you are Republican you are going to follow this agenda, and if you are Democrat, you are going to follow this agenda. And I think that the agenda changes; it changes with the generations and with what America needs, and I think that if you follow one then you are not helping the rest of the people. I hope that I am making sense.

Through her expressed reservations toward party affiliation she reveals the care with which she approaches information. She utilizes the knowledge of others by discussing the election with "a lot" of people. Moreover, she expresses a healthy skepticism about news writers' "perspectives" influencing their reporting, an attitude amplified by subject 1. Subject 1 was employed part time at a telemarketing firm. He was a 20-something causasian male living out of an extra room at his friend's apartment in the northern suburbs of Chicago.

R: What do you think of political ads in general?

S1: I find them highly unnecessary. I mean people shouldn't vote unless they like study what it is they are voting for, and ads don't do very much. I mean they advertise things and stuff on TV all the time, and that doesn't make what they're selling on TV any better. The same goes for political ads.

R: Who do you think studies the candidates more, the people who are highly involved or people who didn't make up their minds already?

S1: Well, by highly involved what do you mean by that?

R: The people who like volunteer for the Republicans, or people who are anti-abortion who go make phone calls at night.

S1: Well, I would assume, like, I remember seeing a lot on the news, you know, there would be like a group of people that would vote for someone like for just one reason. I remember I saw on the news they had like a big group of gay people and they were like, "We're voting for Gore . . . just because we're gay." A lot of people, they seem to do that. They seem to vote for one guy just for one reason and that's it. They don't really seem to study it at all, so I would say that the people that haven't made up their mind probably seem to study it more.

* * *

R: When you are sitting at home, imagine it's before the election and an ad comes on. What is the first thought that comes to your head, no matter who it is?

S1: Oh yeah, another political ad . . . that's basically it. I usually change the channel.

R: Really, you don't care to watch them?

S1: No.

R: Do you think that is kind of cynical?

S1: No, why watch them? How do I even know what they're saying is true? It's just better to study the candidates and the third party media and whatever, even though media itself is kind of biased too though I mean like I would watch like Fox News and they are all Democrats so they were all like pro-Gore; and if you look at like the Tribune, I think it was, it was like Republicans, they were always pro-Bush. I think that was the Tribune, I'm not sure.

His discourse regarding news sources is interesting because it demonstrates both knowledge about the perspectival nature of reporting, and a care used when consuming this information. He does not possess a cynical attitude that would cause him to stop reading newspapers or watching TV news. The same applies to his attitude toward politicians. A cynic would have simply expressed his belief that politicians are unbelievable. Why vote for such a person? Underlying this person's criticism, however, is the presumption that one of the candidates should be president. He explains that while he considers the candidates and their spots unbelievable (presumably a product of candidates doing what they have to do to get elected) there are other sources that one can use to learn more accurately about the candidates and their proposals. None of the subjects seemed too pleased with their conclusions about politicians, but they were not dismayed to the point of being angry or resentful. None of these voters had stopped voting on account of these attitudes. In this case, the voter had negative attitudes toward both candidates, and could provide justification for his reasoning. Nevertheless, he voted.

R: Why did you ultimately choose the candidate you voted for in the last election?

S1: It was a very hard decision and I had to think about it for a long time. Does it matter if I say who I voted for?
R: You can go ahead.

S1: Um, I finally, in the end, voted for Bush. It was such like a toss up—because Gore was pro-environment. And I don't really like Republicans, I'm really *not* a Republican; I'm a Democrat. But I voted for Bush because, I don't know, I guess you can just say I was being paranoid about the big conspiracy thing. But Clinton was, I wouldn't want to have Clinton in the office again and having Gore in there was just a little too close to Clinton and it always seemed like he probably might have knew more things than he did. I'm sure there were a lot of cover-ups, they seem to have done a lot of cover-ups. And I'm sure that he just knows a lot more and probably fought the election so hard because he wanted to win so he could keep the stuff covered up, and um, you know Bush was offering the tax cut and the tax cut is nice.

That he voted for Bush was a surprising disclosure, considering his age and place in life. Struggling to make it as a telemarketer, he did not have much material wealth or comfort; still, his discourse and his vote reflected an enduring optimistic attitude. After entertaining both candidates he ultimately supported the only candidate he perceived would help him materially. Despite his skepticism about the virtues of these two men, he explains that he weighed the relative benefits and drawbacks of both and chose who he believed was the best of the two. Neither candidate was easily dismissed by him.

Subject 21 was another male union firefighter in the far west suburbs of Chicago. He was married with children and lived on a very comfortable salary—no doubt the benefit of union bargaining. His responses reflect an interesting anxiety about information. He describes himself as a late-decider who was fairly certain about which candidate he supported. Judgment was withheld because he believed he needed more information.

R: Um, ultimately why, and you don't have to tell me who you voted for, if you did, it wouldn't help my study one way or the other, but why did you choose the candidate you ultimately voted for?

S21: Um, just through his campaign I heard a lot of positive things. And, um, I know I don't have to tell you, but, like if I listen to Al Gore, I didn't have much faith in the Clinton administration for as long as he was in there. Al Gore was one of them. Now, you might say that he tried separating himself from Clinton but he was still part of those eight years in there. So, it's kind of hard to see what happened over the eight years and say what's going to make him different. So, maybe, what we looked at for the Clinton administration, we looked at, uh, we looked at an ongoing portion of the Clinton administration, but only through Al Gore. So I guess we'd have to be a track record of the administration that Gore was mixed up in, versus somebody who is fresh, even though George Bush's father was president eight years ago.

R: Well, it would appear that you thought Bush was very sincere; you kind of rejected the Clinton administration—why did it take you so long to choose who to vote for?

S21: Uh, I guess to be sure. To be positive, unless I missed something. You can't watch TV 24/7 each day. You can't listen to all the news channels. You know, you never know, maybe you'll read something and you'll pick up on it, but then you might hear somebody else say something that you never thought about. In a good article, an editorial, or an ad or something like that, or even in an article someplace. Maybe a candidate will trip over his own two feet and say something that will contradict what he had said before.

R: Okay, so is it safe to say that if the candidate you supported had a major blunder, you were prepared to vote for the other candidate?

S21: I would have to really waiver my decision for a while and think about it. Um, I would have to really think about what he said and why he said it and probably look a little deeper into more of his campaign in the next week or so and see how that goes.

R: So you weren't so committed to one candidate or the other that you wouldn't have changed your mind during the last week.

S21: Correct.

* * *

R: How would you describe yourself in comparison to what you would consider to be the ideal voter?

S21: How would I concern myself, compare myself to that? To the ideal voter? Well, I'm neither Republican nor Democrat. Um, a lot of people are just strict, you know, one party or the other, regardless of how good, good of a man they are going to be in office. Like a Democrat, if they had a good Republican running, they won't vote for him no matter what. Where I would be willing to weigh both ways and take the better of the two men, or whichever one gets my vote.

R: So, your votes in past presidential elections, you have considered both candidates?

S21: Yes, yes.

R: What role do you think political advertisements play in your decision making?

S21: Not a whole lot. Only because I think the typical politician has a bunch of B.S. behind him to begin with, regardless if you are talking about; presidential, congressional, or small town politics. They are quick and they are brief and I think during the television campaigns they are telling people what they want to hear. So, um, I don't think there are ways of pulling them apart. Maybe it helps clarify something that you may hear later on, to hear them, uh, like the advertisement for the senior citizens, well, I heard what, 30 seconds worth or 45 seconds worth of stuff, well maybe later on I might hear 10, 15, 20 minutes of it. Plus you hear in the debates, after the debates, commercials; some of the commercials come out where each one can clarify what they are talking about. I don't think it's a very good thing.

R: Characterizing ads as telling you what you want to hear sounds kind of negative. What's wrong with that? What do you mean by that?

S21: Uh, both Gore and Bush. Gore, Gore tells me that I want that tax relief. That's what I want to hear. Everybody wants money back, no matter who you are. Middle class, you know, whatever, everybody wants their money back. So, I think he's planning on people to say, "Well, if I vote for Gore in a year I could have $600 back or $500 back." Well, the same thing with Bush, though, you know, we already have a system in place we just have to keep that system going. Whereas Gore is trying to create something new, Bush is just trying to keep reviving what we presently have. And I think that is a much easier fight than me going back and trying to create something new.

Split between candidates and exhibiting little support for the parties, this voter's comments illustrate well the observations made here. He is an optimist but a skeptic (not a cynic). He is withholding judgment in order to discern the "better of the two men" all the while describing them as having "a bunch of B.S. behind" them. He dismisses their ads as "quick" and "brief" but this is not a problem, as there are other sources of information. Though he was leaning toward Bush, he remains undecided—perhaps out of fairness, perhaps out of concern for future information that might better help him discern the "right" candidate, perhaps aware that something new and important might be disclosed making his decision, easier by ruling out one of the options.

The modern objective voter needs more than just evidence that supports his/her voting preference. Instead, this voter needs *enough* evidence. This voting modality is scientific in that it requires controls and criteria in order for the voter to make claims of validity. This concept of scientific voting is the general observation that emerges in this chapter and stemming from this observation is the critique developed in chapters 5 and 6. A true scientist distances him/herself as much as possible from the phenomenon investigated. True science is not social, it is intersubjective. Unfortunately, with all other voting modalities effectively discredited, swing voters are modeling science and disengaging from the public arena. For these voters, presidential politics is decreasingly a domain of public participation; presidential politics is just a period of time between Labor Day and Election Day culminating in a final measurement of public support.

4

A HERMENEUTIC OF MODERN VOTING

> . . . objectivity, whatever its epistemological status, has become the commanding life style of our society: the one most authoritative way of regarding the self, others, and the whole of our enveloping reality. Even if it is not, indeed possible to be objective, it *is* possible so to shape the personality that it will feel and act *as if* one were an objective observer and to treat everything that experience presents to the person in accordance with what objectivity would seem to demand.
> Theodore Roszak (1969)

CHARACTERISTICS AND ORIGINS OF MODERN SWING VOTING

The previous chapter described characteristics central to the modern swing voter: They vote out of a sense of obligation, are politically unplugged, less impassioned about their decisions, and they strive to be objective. In a sense, these voters are a blend of both conservative and liberal suppositions; they attempt to learn who the "right" candidate is (an empirical truth "out there") without trying to impose a particular order on the country. Political conservatives are quite different insofar as they possess predispositions regarding a permanent order that society should emulate; they favor candidates who promote a similar order. More humanistic liberals, on the other hand, tend to reject the notion of an absolute truth "out there." Viewed by liberals as fascistic, the notion of legislating monolithic order is considered by them to be dangerous for a free and democratic society. Generally, they believe that one person or group should not be caused to live according to another's notion of a right or true order; individuals should be allowed to determine for themselves their own life trajectories: "I want to make money," "I want to be a dancer," "I want to be a poet." From the humanist vantage point, sociological factors which impede self-determination are harmful and should be remedied.

Certainly, the conservative and liberal conceptions just described preceded the phenomenon of swing voting I've described. In the historical struggle to wrest power from tyrants, despots, and monarchs lies the origin of our contemporary partisan conceptualizations. Evidence of this struggle is implicit in the words used to describe the parties as either "liberal" or "conservative." In 1996, Senator Bob Dole offered during his Republican nomination speech to be the nation's "bridge to the past," that is, to conserve a prior order that many judged right or proper. Consistent with its Latin meaning (*conservare*), the conservative seeks to *preserve* the system. Liberals (the root of which is the Latin *liber* meaning "free"), on the other hand, struggle to overcome these older conventions in order to *liber*-ate themselves or others. Men and women of the 60s singing "We Shall Overcome" were seeking to defeat prejudicial and seemingly arbitrary laws believed harmful to racial and ethnic minorities and underrepresented groups.

Despite their purposes and meanings, voter interest in political parties continues to wane. Sabato (1988) pointed out more than a decade ago that:

> Before the 1950's, while evidence is more circumstantial because of the scarcity of reliable survey research data, there are indications that Independents were many fewer in number, and party loyalties considerably firmer. (p. 112)

He continues, explaining that today's picture is much different.

> Being a socially acceptable, integrated, and contributing member of one's community once almost demanded partisan affiliation; it was a badge of good citizenship, motherhood, and apple pie, signifying that one was a patriot. Today the labels are shunned as an offense to a thinking person's individualism, and a vast majority of Americans insist they vote for "the man, not the party." (p. 117)

To understand *how* this change happened, it is important to understand *what* has happened. The rejection of party (perceived by many as a limiting, instead of a facilitating institution) and the growth of self interpretation as a value is a manifestation of a much more significant societal shift.

Knowing the history out of which these manifestations of social change emerged helps us to understand more specifically what these changes mean. Generally, this chapter and chapter 5 argue that swing voters are influenced by a general trend away from the valuing, or understanding for that matter, of the public sphere. The public sphere and the conventions that govern it have fallen into such a state of disrepair that many voters are completely unequipped to function "publicly" within it. The society of the United States fails to value and perpetuate the social conventions necessary for individuals to participate in the public domain, or to value or respect the participation of others. From the "middle," parties are devalued, politicians ridiculed, partisans considered extremists, and participation beyond voting believed the byproduct of naïve idealism. In lieu of partisan politics, we are encouraged to "keep it real," to govern our lives according to the dictates of the private sphere. When the time comes to vote, however, it is nearly impossible to find acceptable ground on which to make judgments. Swing voters possess no functional approach to making *social* sense of the campaign communication environment. With a sense of obligation to something larger than their singularity, swing voters participate by rejecting what they perceive as their subjective instincts, but they have little with which to replace it. They simply attempt to divorce *themselves* from their decision: this constitutes contemporary public behavior. They are hyperobjective or deficiently rational. As a result they seriously limit themselves in their ability to pass judgment on candidates or policy. Public and political social conventions once provided a functional and practical inbetween, enabling people to reconcile their own beliefs and domestic needs with those of their community. As with the understanding of public conventions, this ability has diminished.

DIMENSIONAL ACCRUAL/DISSOCIATION THEORY

To tender a complaint that swing voters function in too modern or too objective a manner seems at first to be counterintuitive. This notion of modern voting seems desirable. Given the connotative loadings on language like *modern, scientific*, and *objective* it seems swing voters exemplify our society's conceptualization of the ideal voter. According to this line of reasoning it might seem that the general characteristics of swing voting described in the previous chapter (making careful, emotionally detached, distanced, and measured voting decisions without prejudice) are better voters than their partisan counterparts. The following section brackets these value judgments, considering them in light of Kramer's (1997) dimensional accrual/dissociation theory. Kramer maintains that the attitudes of these voters make manifest the attitudes of deficient-rationality marked by hyperanxiety over method, certitude, and efficiency (measure).

Influenced by the cultural hermeneutic of Gebser (1949/1985), Kramer (1997) maintains that, as dimensions of consciousness accrue, the world becomes more distanced and we more dissociated from it. As ego emerged within earlier cultures, for example, consciousness separated self and tribe from the world in which it was enmeshed. According to this mode of consciousness I am no longer a part of the world but am instead a self in the world. Along with these feint glimmerings of self and will come the seeds of the abstraction of the Earth and the rationale for subjecting it to our will, regardless of the costs. This is the distanciation that Kramer argues accompanies the accrual of dimensions. The dimensions include those of self or ego (as opposed to nature), time, and space. As consciousness continues to unfold throughout a culture's development, these dimensions are accrued. Time, once incomprehensible (for the pejoratively named cave-man), is today understood in a completely modern fashion marked by the abstract spatialization and commodification outlined at length by Edward Hall (1990). We think and speak of a timeline possessing a past and a future divided by now. Time is further divided into discreet moments. Like any empirical commodity, time can be spent, wasted, and saved. This way of thinking about time enables modern future orientation as opposed to living in the present. Future-oriented cultures live in or toward the future, and inhabit less the concrete world of the present. Perhaps no one has better summed up the Western notion of time orientation than John Lennon who explained that, "Life is what happens while you are busy making plans." A truly future-oriented person distances her/himself from the concrete, immediate, and consequently more visceral present to best control her/his future. My friend tells me, "It's been a long time since I've had guilt-free time." Though not empirically present, a future goal shades his present moments as he psychically exists both now and in the future.

Kramer (1997) explains that as "dimensionality increases, so too does dissociation in all its forms, including emotional and semantic detachment from concrete expression" (p. xiii). It is found that more dissociated modern Western nations typically celebrate the masculine virtues of control, discipline, and aloofness. This is best exemplified by the 19th-century English notion that one should keep a stiff upper lip in order to avoid emotional display betraying weakness.

Understanding Gebser's (1949/1985) notion of the dimensioning of consciousness helps us comprehend better "where" we are in terms of culture. Phenomenologically speaking, humans are cultural animals that intend their world. How we synthesize the world is determined by the cultural understanding of the self in the world developed by culture as it adapted to exigencies. Adapted from Herbert Spencer's notion of evolution and mutation, similar to the development of organisms, consciousness modalities evolve or mutate as ways of waring are accrued rather than shed. As one modality becomes deficient due to a culture's awakening the culture awakens to the need for greater dimensioning, not replacing but building on the prior modality. The prior modality remains, it is just built upon. Still, it is sedimented—unacknowledged by consciousness. In order, Gebser (1949/1985) terms these modalities, "archaic," "magic," "mythic," "mental," and "integral"; they represent an unfolding of consciousness. Cultural development "forward"[1] from one modality to another is a "plus mutation" enabling the culture to function more efficaciously in the environment (cultural as well as physical) in which it finds itself, overcoming the limitations or failings of the prior mode of consciousness.[2]

Gebser's (1949/1985) "mental" consciousness modality is equated here with "modernity." This modern mode of consciousness is the prevailing structuration of consciousness among Western societies. This manner of intending the world is characterized as "perspectival," "rational," and three dimensional. Indicative of this mode of awareness is the privileging of individual perspective as evidenced in Renaissance painting. Realist art attempts to depict depth, but does so from the perspective of the individual painter. The truth of the images painted are no longer determined by the way the images depict relationships and order. Instead, truth *is* as perceived by the individual. We can check their accuracy by assuming their perspective, making certain the images and the object correspond. Gebser explains the development of modernity:

> This process is an extraordinary event which is literally earth-shaking; it bursts man's protective psychic circle and congruity with the psychic-naturalistic-cosmic-temporal world of polarity and enclosure. The ring is broken, and man steps out of the two-dimensional surface into space, which he will attempt to master by his thinking. (p. 75)

The significance of this modern consciousness modality is that the individual's perspective is privileged. The world "out there" is presupposed to be equally accessible to all. Privileging the individual is not the same as valuing subjectivity. Instead, it means that objectivity was a possibility. The individual was privileged *over* some authority or myth. Thus, individual observations of the world could be valid provided that, despite scrutiny, it attained intersubjective agreement. The same world was out there for all to see. Authority was transferred from that/those believed to inherently possess it (e.g., scripture, clergy, and monarchs) to those whose ideas or empirical observations withstood dialectical verification.

---

[1] Despite its limitations, linear language is used here to suggest more of an enhanced complexity rather than an improvement.

[2] Gebser (1949/1985) notes that cultures can move backward, in a 'minus mutation.'

With dimensional accrual comes dissociation. Dissociation can be construed as a separation from both world and the collective (the community). The dissociated individual resides *amongst* an aggregate as opposed to living *within* a community. The dissociated individual is well exemplified by a friend who tells me, "I've decided that having children is not going to change my life," as if the outcome were entirely a matter of will. Her comment emerged from a discussion about her decision to both have children and work full-time as a CPA in an accounting firm—a job that requires her to work 60 hours per week or more, depending on the season. Clearly, her statement is grounded in the presupposition that the individual is capable of living a life that is separate from the lives and needs of others. It pretends that an interconnection does not exist between self and others, absolving the individual of obligation to others while enabling the self to extol its accomplishments as solely its own. The moment-to-moment attention of the mother is substituted by, perhaps, a nanny; a stranger willing to exchange his/her time and effort offering the child some approximation of loving care in exchange for abstract units of value.

On a larger scale, dissociation is found to manifest at the cultural level. To the extent that the public sphere as conceived by Habermas (1962/1989) and the private sphere have collapsed into one another, this is maintained to be true. No longer are the generally accepted social conventions of the public sphere celebrated or imposed as they once were. Dress codes are generally a thing of the past. Images of people "hitting the town" in suits or gowns have been replaced by T-shirts, gym shoes, and fanny packs. Few churches I've attended (which have been mostly Roman Catholic) require attendees to dress nicely. The attitude in these churches is one of "whatever will grow the flock," or at least reduce the flock's hemorrhaging. The reasoning that one need not give their clothing to God if He already has their heart is sound enough. No Christian maintains that an individual achieves grace through their wardrobe. The desire *not* to dress nicely is indicative of a larger social move wherein there are fewer occasions worthy of extraordinary dress. *Reasoning* not to dress nicely because one doesn't have to evidences a mode of reasoning fundamentally different from *feeling* that one must dress up in God's house. According to this reasoning, one's manner of dress is dictated by one's desires and not by external mores or standards. Erin Brockovich taught us that the way a person dresses does not accurately reflect the worth of the person. Her story's success is attributed to the popular U.S. myth that one can pull oneself up by the bootstraps without changing one's boots. The nouveaux riche, David Brook's (2000) bourgeois Bohemians, no longer try to blend with old money. Multimillionaire gangster wrappers work hard to foster the impression that they have both succeeded yet not sold out by continuing to dress in the "fashions" that reflect their more humble upbringings. Many in fact produce their own clothes. Today, it is difficult to say that people eschew social clothing standards, because it is quite likely that they are ignorant of them altogether. Is anyone left besides Emily Post and her daughter who know how to properly dress for a formal dinner, an interview, or work?

Similarly, rules for public interaction and deliberation have collapsed along with respect for the institutions that foster such things. The United States, characterized as a horizontal society (Triandis, 1995), tends generally to view all individuals as relatively equal—an atomistic notion characteristic of much of Western modernity. In such a society, boundaries collapse and all people are fair game for approach and confrontation. This, however, is the recipe for liberation and not deliberation, Jerry Springer style aggressiveness and not discourse in a safe forum. Civil disobedience loses its ability to attract attention when it becomes the norm, thus it is no longer news to learn that our leaders have been heckled. Acts of disobedience become more outrageous: Prime Minister Tony Blair is assaulted by purple powder, Arnold Schwarzenegger pelted with a raw egg, President George H.W. Bush followed and harassed by a man in a chicken outfit, and former Illinois Governor Ryan smashed in the face with a pie. Quite a bit has changed; historian Kenneth Ackerman (2003) explains that press reports of President Garfield's health following his shooting constituted the first time the personal life of the president was considered newsworthy. Until that point, he was considered a *public* figure, a distinction that afforded definite boundaries; the president's private life was off limits. There were no explicit rules separating public from private, just implicit standards understood and respected without their having to be overtly expressed. The distance once afforded to public officials, once granted, is now *imposed* by the Secret Service who have been protecting the president since 1894 (it is noteworthy that it has not always existed). Today, the president must tell the press that his daughters are off limits, and still there is no guarantee that they will not be exploited by the media.

Regarding political participation, the same phenomenon exists; the private individualistic sphere has overcome the public sphere. Habermas (1962/1989) argued that the behavioral expectations of these two spheres are distinct, evolving, and designed to perform two different functions. Sennett (1976) maintains that the public sphere has "fallen" or devolved to such a point as to have been overcome by the more emotive "rules" determining private behavior. The crux of the arguments explaining the attitudes in the previous chapter rely on this distinction. The complex web of meaningful social behaviors that once constituted the mode of interaction in the public sphere has been largely lost. As with other social functions, voters have misplaced an understanding or appreciation of the value of political parties as institutions that facilitate the advocacy and compromise of competing social ideals and interests. When it comes time to vote, without knowledge or appreciation of these nuanced institutions, they assume a quasiscientific approach or "objective personality" (Mumford, 1934) to voting. Mumford explains:

> . . . between the personality that was most effective in the technically immature environment of the tenth century and the type that is effective today, one may say that the first was subjectively [emotionally][3] conditioned, and that the second is more directly influenced by objective situations. These, at all events, seem to be the tendencies. In both types of personality there was an external standard of reference: but whereas the medieval man determined reality by the extent to which it agreed with a complicated tissue of beliefs, in the case of modern man the final arbiter of judgment is always a set of facts, recourse to which is equally open and equally satisfactory to all normally constituted organisms. (pp. 360–361)

For the modern person (or voter) the "complicated tissue of beliefs" is missing or irrelevant. Generally, public beliefs, standards, or conventions are interpreted as arbitrary and restrictive; conventions limit the ego—*me!* No longer functioning in the public sphere, people are unfamiliar with its purpose or requirements. Political institutions shaped and honed by people adapting to historical exigencies, political threats, and social pressures are snubbed. Untrained in the social nuances of the public sphere, swing voters rely on the few familiar rules they trust are socially sanctioned; the modern swing voter pursues "pure fact" as evidenced by the information fixation of the voters included in this study.

TRACING THE ORIGINS OF THE MODERN SWING-VOTER ATTITUDE

From what experience or consciousness modality does the modern swing-voter attitude emerge? Answering this question helps us better understand the very nature of the attitude possessed by swing voters. It is in contrast to Gebser's (1949/1985) notion of the mythic consciousness that democracy and modern voting are best comprehended. Gebser's (1949/1985) notion of the unfolding consciousness posits that the mythic modality precedes and co-presents with modern perspectivity. This is a somewhat relativistic notion that alternative modes of knowing (none of which are privileged by this project) exist.

Specifically, Gebser (1949/1985) explains that modern consciousness is a cultural accomplishment, a step further out of nature. Advancement in human ability to see itself (as a collective cultural unit) as separate from the world, something we moderns take for granted, spatializes our modern rational understanding of the world. The modern modality of consciousness enables us to view the world as an enemy or as a force to conquer. Though this attitude certainly has contributed to terrible environmental stresses, it is

---

[3]Bracketed remark is my own.

this abstracting mentality with its linearity and sequentializing organization that allows us to question and subdue natural forces to our quantifiable advantage—some for the benefit of all and some for very individual purposes. Thus, children are vaccinated, beef irradiated, water chlorinated and dammed; wars are waged for oil and rainforests destroyed for hardwoods. Unfolding as polar dimensioning is mythic consciousness. Mythic waring is marked by an awakening to time; it realizes an earthly rhythm as the seasons are acknowledged for their cyclical nature with their ebbs and flows. The culture is not yet future oriented as time has not yet been abstracted from the natural cycles of the planet—time just is. Each day in time follows a rhythm with a crest and a valley or day and night. Time, the day, the season, each has polarity, or a figurative light and dark. Mythic thought is marked by this polarity, though it is co-present with our own modern waring. With good there is bad, gods are coupled with devils, and males and females complete a whole; polarity colors all things intended by the mythic consciousness. Just as myth implies, cultural consciousness lives the occurrences of the world as matters of coincidence or "rhythmic perchances." These occurrences are explicable; myths or stories are uttered to give meaning and, in a polar devotion, predictability to a circular world.

Evidenced in the mythic structure is the distanciation or dissociation noted by Kramer (1997); mythic waring marks the emergence of human consciousness. The dim flickerings of the will, mind, and imagination begin to stand out against the backdrop of the environment it inhabits.

> The mythical structure is distinct from the magic [premythic] in that it bears the stamp of imagination . . . , rather than the stress of emotion. In the magic structure, the vital connections reach awareness and are manifested in emotional forms: in actions dominated by impulse and instinct and subordinate to the demands and ramifications of spontaneous, affective reactions such as sympathy and antipathy. . . . [The magic structure] is spaceless and timeless, and has an emotional and instinctual consciousness responsive to the demands of nature and the earth. The mythical structure, however . . . has an imaginatory consciousness, reflected in the imagistic nature of myth and responsive to the soul and sky of the ancient cosmos. (Gebser, 1949/1985, p. 67)

The image-ination (imagining) evidences the beginnings or abstract awareness—the mind occupied by notions other than the immediate, concrete, or visceral. The imaginatory consciousness is not yet fully conscious or aware in a modern or rational way of the world it inhabits. The stories told and passed along are understood by us as "collective dreams" simply put to words, though the same stories constituted for them embodied psychic realities.

It would not occur to early mythic culture to question its understandings of its world. Gebser (1949/1985) explains that mythic consciousness is still "pre-perspectival" meaning the individual ego is not yet positioned in the world with its focus on the world emanating from its own view. Trusting one's own perspective or observations similar to the ways of the realist painter, as opposed to the seemingly naturally occurring myths emanating from the world, is more di*mensioned* than polar reality and holds the possibility of multiple perspectives—something radical (and even frightening) to those unaware of the grip some contemporary myth is wielding. Mumford (1951) discusses the nature of cultural myths:

> Man has told himself many stories about his origin and his destination. Two things are common to these myths: they reflect, with simple childlike unconsciousness, the humble details of his daily life; and they recognize the existence of agents and forces he has never beheld with his eyes or seized with his hand . . . (p. 62)

Earlier mythic culture simply *pre*-existed emanating from individual life experiences shared communally in the culture or was passed along through the generations as stories and "rules" of conduct. Today we have more immediate resources of myth through multiple forms of media whose agents are also invisible.

Ong (1982) makes clear the point that myth springs forth from human experience because there is little recourse to anything else. Mythic culture is culture of the *mouth* (the two are etymologically linked); it is uttered and heard, not written. The limits of mythic reasoning are determined by the very nature of spoken discourse: fleeting, time-bound to the here and now, and influential because it is perceived as true. The notion of "wrong" arises when one is comparing among possibilities; with mythic thought there is less likelihood of this comparison and it would be a comparison of stories rather than of empirical facts. "In the total absence of any writing, there is nothing outside the thinker, no text, to enable him or her to produce the same line of thought again or even to verify whether he or she has done so or not" (Ong, 1982, p. 34).

Historically, any statement worth handing down was put to verse. Texts such as the Torah and the works attributed to Homer (*The Iliad* and *The Odyssey*) utilized rhythm, rhyme, and other mnemonic devices to enable people to commit their stories to memory. The adages and proverbs of today were the governing logics of earlier mythic cultures. Ong (1980) notes that maxims similar to the quaint phrases we teach today's children (e.g., a leopard cannot change his spots; it is better to give than to receive) were used by tribal chiefs to settle disputes and to levy justice. These proverbs were applied as they best fit the situation, sometimes being rejected by the parties involved only to be replaced until all agreed. We see this approach in the Old Testament story of Solomon who offered to divide a disputed child (1 Kings

3:25). What was *right* in cases such as these was situationally determined.[4] Good "law" was not that which was absolutely right and fair, as we moderns largely quantify it today. With a mythical attunement to situation, communal harmony, as opposed to control, is the measure of juridical success.

By the end of the Middle Ages, mythic waring as the primary cultural mode had become deficient, failing to explain the types of problems faced by people or offering solutions. Mythic consciousness had become a regime imposed by the Holy Roman Empire. Mumford (1934) explains that this period was a valueless one. Popes felt threatened by the growing notion of individualism as expressed in religion and governance, as evidenced by the church's reaction to the publishing of the Bible in the vernacular. People of the day grew tired of the regime:

> From the fifteenth century to the seventeenth men lived in an empty world: a world that was daily growing emptier. They said their prayers, they repeated their formulas, they even sought to retrieve the holiness they had lost by resurrecting superstitions they had long abandon: hence the fierceness and hollow fanaticism of the Counter-Reformation, its burning of heretics, its persecution of witches, precisely in the midst of the growing enlightenment. (pp. 44-45)

As tightly as the church held on, changes were still in the making. Typography, capitalism, Protestantism, all contributed to the firming hold of the modern consciousness modality.

The Shift to Modernity

The Renaissance marked a significant point in the development of European thought. On a scale larger than had been previously witnessed in ancient Greece, Europeans were increasingly willing to trust their own observations and judgments. Specifically, the result of the deficiency of mythic consciousness is that the individual ego and will began to develop; humans stepped even further out of nature. This is well illustrated by Luther's (1990) treatises in which he asked if unordained men should be capable of functioning as their own priests if circumstances denied access to one. Questions like these and their subsequent answers coupled with direct access to scripture each helped decenter the Catholic Church in the lives of the individuals.

---

[4]For instance, a California jury acquitted the police officers accused of beating Rodney King. Regardless of one's thoughts about the verdict, the second "verdict" was handed down by the public which quickly responded with riots. The first verdict considered the situational factors surrounding the beating, while the public's verdict reflected the sense of discord (disharmony) experienced by many in response to the decision.

Without the church's monolithic mythos, individuals were themselves empowered to dis-cover the world that lay hidden behind a waring told in stories to one comprehended in relationships and facts. This was the advent of cultural perspectivism that had been gradually developing in some individuals through the ages (Gebser, 1949/1985). Perspectivism manifests itself throughout Western culture; one is made easily aware of its evolution by examining the changes in art of that period right up until today. Just as art patrons of the Renaissance valued realism, today's consumer demands a standard of realism beyond the unaided eye's ability to scrutinize it (the mega pixel). The quality of digital cameras, computer monitors, and flat screen televisions is determined by their ability to replicate true images. Perspectivism or rationalism fundamentally altered how the individual constituted his/her lifeworld. The modern art movement, for instance, furthers the celebration of the ego and emphasizes truth as determined by the producer of the art, rejecting the notion that art quality is determined by the extent to which it replicates intersubjectively experienced phenomena.

Perspectivism implies a further distanciation or detachment from nature: the modern person becomes as Giedion (1962) terms him/her, "thinking man" as opposed to "feeling man." Finding its etymological roots in the Latin word "ratio," the rational man is analytical and detached, measuring the world, sizing it up, and breaking it down in a manner that takes the world as his own. Each individual is presumed capable of breaking the world down from a whole into its essential parts or into a ratio. By doing this, the world and its governing dynamics can be best understood and hopefully controlled. The rational approach to understanding the world functions best when one is unbiased, objective, and unfettered by traditionalisms.[5]

Although this modern mode of consciousness shook the foundations of the Roman Catholic Church, modernity also forced fundamental changes in Western governmental arrangements (for related reasons). From the assumptions of modernism and rationalism, democracy took hold. Provided one conducted enough analysis with an acceptable method, it was understood that the true nature of things was accessible. For democracy, the same principle applied. Provided a society practiced democracy in pure enough form, what was right could be determined. Rousseau's (1762/1978) writing makes apparent the belief that what was thought true for science suitably applied to democracy. Society's common interests, he explained, are "always constant, unalterable and pure." He adds:

> As long as several men in assembly regard themselves as a single body, they have only a single will which is concerned with their common preservation and general well-being. In this case, all the springs of the State are vigorous and simple and its rules clear and luminous;

---

[5]As Roszak (1969) and others argue, this is often *also* a myth.

> there are no embroilments or conflicts of interests; the common good is everywhere clearly apparent, and only good sense is needed to perceive it. (p. 73)

This sentiment exists more than one hundred years later, as Peirce (1871) explains:

> . . . human opinion universally tends in the long run to a definite form, which is the truth. Let any human being have enough information and exert enough thought upon any question, and the result will be that he will arrive at a certain definite conclusion, which is the same that any other mind will reach under sufficiently favorable circumstances. (p. 455)

Similar to understanding the apodictic laws of the physical universe, Peirce argues that the general will of a people is determinable by any one of its members. Attitudes like these constitute the basis upon which democracy was predicated: if there existed no uniform will, humanity would continue to need the guidance of an authority.

MODERN TIME AND ETERNAL TRUTHS

> . . . it is still a metaphysical faith upon which our faith in science rests—that even we seekers after knowledge today . . . take our fire, too, from the flame lit by a faith that is thousands of years old, that Christian faith which was also the faith of Plato, that God is the truth, that truth is divine.
> Nietzsche (1887, 1974)

Today's three-strikes laws have become a lightening rod for many critics. These laws are mandatory-sentencing policies that remove from the presiding judge the ability to determine proper sentencing. The center of the argument regarding these laws revolves around whether one believes these laws should exist at all. Does a person arrested for swiping videos from K-Mart, Leandro Andrade's third felony or "strike," deserve to serve 50 years to life in prison with no possibility of parole before he serves 50 years, regardless of the discretion of the judge (Gearan, 2003)? The Supreme Court upheld the law, though many agree that automatically granting this man a sentence typically reserved for murder is a bit excessive. But should the specific facts of the case count? After all, a law is a law, right?

This case illustrates the ontological clash between relativists and absolutists. Those wishing to overturn these laws have a relativistic perspective, believing that an examination of the circumstances surrounding the incident is essential for determining proper sentencing. Time plays a role here. What happened *then*, when Mr. Andrade committed his felony, matters. Those circumstances contextualize and constitute the nature of the act. On the other hand, the absolutist position is *time-less*. The how, when, and why of the felonious act are irrelevant. Referencing situation-less, context-less, and absolute laws, the state of California need only recognize the offender as a recidivist felon to determine that he is a social risk. The human judge, implicitly considered by California to be inadequately consistent in his/her judgment, perhaps as an unfortunate result of human sympathies and consideration of transitory concerns, is superseded by the California legal apparatus. The system is closed. The legal apparatus in this instance is automatic—just flip the switch and clear the dockets.[6]

The case of the three-strikes laws exemplifies how the modern ontological presuppositions of science encroach on social attitudes. Public policy and politics are domains that are influenced by scientific presuppositions. Relevant to this project is the argument that the notion of timeless apodictic law has pervaded political reasoning and voting practices. It has displaced the seemingly "less-exacting" conventions of public behavior with more standardized and "rational" practice. The technical and descriptive "it is" replaces the more transitory and situational "it seems"; the former extracts individual and social agency and responsibility. With such an abject objectivity, the individual is less necessary under these conditions. As a result, the system becomes less subjective, more objectivizing, repetitious, and static.

The origins of this notion of timeless law and truth are explained by Gebser's (1949/1985) notion of the magic consciousness. Magic time as a single-pointedness of experience is a common experience of time's dimensioning. People were not conscious of eternity but without the influences of modern ideas of transitory time, this moment is no different than the previous moment—in fact there is no notion of moment or movement at all (this division is a modern contrivance). Time isn't *passing*: I just am. In this mode of consciousness, there was a presumption of completeness. Everything was right, a part of the whole.

The Old Testament story of Adam and Eve ends with both being evicted from paradise. Previously destined to live eternally in the garden of Eden, they were evicted (time was up) into a transitory world in which they would die: sentenced to exist in time's duration of moment following on moment—a conceivably lighter sentence than Mr. Andrade's *hard* time. This story, more than just a story, reflects a cultural attitude that considers fleeting or contingent phenomena as lesser-than; banishment into the transitory is considered a punishment. The Christian goal is to reunite with eternity—to pass out of the transitory and into an eternity characterized by Christianity and influenced by Plato as a state of perfection. The story also makes evident that as

---

[6]This move alone evidences society's reliance upon technology (techne) toward a totalizing efficiency—magic.

time irrupted into consciousness (as violent as Adam and Eve's eviction), humans were unwilling to relinquish the notion of the eternal and perfect, the state of undimensioned waring from which temporally aware cultures emerged. Though relativistic notions of time have begun to alter late modernism's notion of time, the premodernistic notions of time still govern how many continue to conceive of and cope with our situatedness; magical and mythical dimensions are ever-present possibilities with degrees of appropriateness in time's plural dimensions. Our contemporary perspective conceives of transitory time as a monolithic time (clock time), which everyone experiences in a presumably uniform way. Five minutes on my Bulova are the same five minutes on Big Ben, just check with Cesium Fountain Atomic Clock at the National Institute of Standards and Technology and see for yourself. Although we share this monolithic and transitory time with its beginnings and endings, its punch clocks and stop watches, there also exists the conceived realm of the timeless. Whether God exists there or not is subject to argument, though little doubt exists, however, that the timeless is constituted by the eternal and unwavering rules that govern our world.

The modern notion of time emerged in Western society in the fourteenth century as a result of Christian anxiety about order, as prayer needed to be regulated and timely. Prior to this, the idea that time existed and passed was present in awareness, but the procession of time was governed by nature. Time had rhythm, but it was not yet a quantity. With the advent of the clock, time became a constant and specialized phenomenon. The commodification of time emerged: it could run out, be wasted, or used up. That time could run out was truly a limitation of this world in contrast to the timeless. Mumford (1934) also notes that the clock helped develop throughout western culture the firm belief in an "independent world of mathematically measurable sequences" (p. 15). That independent world is where constant and immutable laws were thought to reside. These are the pursuits of science. Priests were once thought to be intermediaries between planes of the time-bound and timeless. Men were ordained as priests following rigorous training in self-denial; prior to Vatican II, the priest stood at the front of the church with his back to the parishioners speaking to God on the congregation's behalf. The congregation looked to the priest. Ironically similar are the practices of scientists; they also learn to strip themselves of their subjectivities in order to best access the timeless rules of nature. They look at the protons, planets, plants, and people. We, in turn, look to them.

The notion of an "independent world of mathematically measurable sequences" is central to all modern scientific endeavors. All of science attempts to reduce to formulas the dynamics and forces that govern our world, thus rendering it predictable. The clock allows me to predict when my students will convene in my classroom. Told to be present at 9:00 A.M., about 90% arrive shortly beforehand while the rest will either saunter in late or stay home. Similarly, knowing the temperature, barometric pressure, and humidity can help predict storms with some certainty. Explaining science, Leibniz (1714/1998) states, "True reasoning depends on necessary or *eternal truths* like those of logic, numbers, and geometry, which makes indubitable connections between ideas, and conclusions which are inevitable." Even more to the point, he adds that the pursuit of "eternal truths is what distinguishes us from mere animals . . . And that is what in us is called a rational soul, or a mind." The assumption of the existence and accessibility of timeless apodictic principles is the foundation for scientific theory building.

Evidence of this world's governing principles existed not in us (the subjective), but out there in the world (the objective). Provided the observers could sufficiently bracket their assumptions regarding the functioning of our world, they could access the knowledge of the timeless dynamics that govern it. Trips to the moon, conception by sixty-year-old women, and genetic engineering leave very little doubt that this approach has been very successful in the physical and biological sciences. But what was successful early with physical science was quickly applied to human life (social engineering). As evidenced in Mr. Andrade's story, even jurisprudence is subjected to science's faith in immutable rules.

The language and presumptions of science have helped shape modern approaches to many things, including politics. As pointed out, implicit in the discourse of the voters interviewed in this study is the belief that among the available candidates, one of them is best. One need only strip themselves of partisan biases and eschew conventions and view the election objectively. Today, these notions shape the public participation of our swing voters.

INSTITUTIONALIZATION OF MODERN VOTING PARTICIPATION

Voting is characterized by the assumptions constituting it as a collective act practiced to access and realize the common interests of the people of a nation; it is performed to determine what is the right or best course. Today, we criticize the voting practices in early U.S. history because they were largely exclusionary, privileging only Caucasian, male, landowners. For the time, however, that design was revolutionary *because* of its progressiveness, and it wasn't until much later that the nations of Europe caught up to the advancements of the United States. The intent was to enfranchise those considered, within the cultural system of that time, the most reasoned, educated, and vested. These citizens, it was believed, could determine what was best for the society.

The democratic notion of the equal citizen is what has catalyzed much of the change in institutionalized voting practices in the United States. This equality is what Kramer (1997) terms the "perspectival law of equivalences." He explains, "Each part is identical and therefore interchangeable with each other part" (p. xvi). Thus, what follows in U.S. history is an improvement of the U.S. democracy as citizens are, as a matter of practice, recognized and treated more equally before the law. The expansion of enfranchisement and more scientific voting practices were the methods used to help make expression as uninfluenced from external sources as possible.

Early on, the notion of universal suffrage made little sense. It is ridiculous to think geographers would require the agreement of the earth's population, much less its majority, in order to verify the Earth's spherical shape. Likewise, it was believed that a comprehensive vote was unnecessary to tap the "single will" of a society. Even the expansion of suffrage was not intended as a move toward a multivocal society or a nation with universal enfranchisement. Instead, the denial of voting rights (to any white males) made little sense in light of the assumed ability of the individual to reason. Schudson (1998) documents the states' expansion of voting rights from property-owning caucasian males to all tax-paying caucasian males. He explains that this extension of rights was based on the assumption that property owners *and* earners would reason well enough to respect the right of property.

Schudson (1994) describes the stark contrast between contemporary voting and early voting in the United States. Many of the voting practices we take for granted would have been considered frivolous luxuries by the standards of the eighteenth century. "The . . . jealously guarded privacy of voting today contrasts dramatically with the viva voce process of the eighteenth century Virginia or the colorful party ticket voting of the nineteenth century" (p. 61). At the founding of this nation, enfranchised people publicly voted and participated in parades. Traveling to vote, often many miles away in rural areas, was an exciting occasion (Schudson, 1998).

Many of the adaptations to the voting process were realized between 1865 and 1920 because of the reform efforts of the Mugwumps and Progressives (Schudson, 1998). For instance, at the turn of the nineteenth century, political parties did not rely on private contributions, as we think of them today, to operate. The political machine was run by assessments and patronage. People who were given government jobs knew that their continued employment was contingent upon the success of party candidates. For this reason, party faithfuls continued to work for campaigns and provided money to the party through assessments on government-derived incomes. In 1877, President Hayes signed an Executive Order enforcing antipolitical assessment legislation threatening to enforce existent laws that outlawed involuntary garnishing of wages by political parties. Following the shooting of President Garfield by a disgruntled government job seeker, President Chester Allen Arthur signed the Pendleton Act of 1883, requiring the use of competitive exams for government job placement (Schudson, 1998). Schudson contends that this type of legislation weakened parties and weakened U.S. democracy: "In the lingering demise of patronage, the musculature of American democracy weakened, and the flesh that made the constitutional bones move in synchrony, if only in certain directions, went slack" (p. 155).

Without patronage, parties had a more difficult time motivating people to participate in the electoral process.

Among the many Jim Crow laws that scar the historical landscape of Southern politics are those requiring passing scores on reading and intelligence tests for voting privileges; today they are considered a repugnant and disenfranchising ploy. Interestingly, these tests were originally employed as suffrage reforms intended to extend the right to vote beyond propertied people. During the nineteenth century, the Mugwumps were challenging the notion of the natural right to vote, which limited voting to those who had inherent qualities (e.g., race, sex, property), maintaining that people who were morally fit and literate should be allowed to vote. The result was that the ability to reason, and thus vote, was determined with a test (Schudson, 1998). In some states, the privilege of voting was extended from landowning white men to white men with passing scores.

Emphasis on direct popular voting also increased during the turn of the century. The seventeenth amendment required the direct election of senators by popular vote (Schudson, 1998). States also began requiring direct primaries. Both of these reforms made parties less important in the political process by putting more power of choice into the hands of the individual voter. Primary reforms continue today, and the same trend toward increased primary significance and voter choice characterizes these movements. In 1969 the McGovern-Fraser Commission, convened to reform the Democratic Party, required primary and caucus delegates to support the candidate to whom they'd sworn allegiance. The result was to strip the power to nominate presidential candidates from party leadership and hand it directly to the electorate (Patterson, 1994).

When voters cast their ballots, even the manner with which they do it has been subject to reform, making the practice largely different than it was 100 years ago. Today, this has been made evident by the efforts following the 2000 election to make vote-recording methods more accurate. Similar concerns emerged much earlier, however. Starting in 1888, states began to use the anonymous Australian-ballot[7] (Schudson, 1998). General presumption today maintains that voting is naturally an anonymous activity, and yet it is not only a relatively recent development in the history of voting, but champions of our democracy at the time of its inception argued *against* the Australian-ballot. Although the reforms that brought about the utilization of the Australian-ballot were intended to counter influence at the polls, public participation through voting became an even more socially sterile activity because the single most important act of civic duty retreated into the voting booth. With this change, voting became a celebration of the private individual making rational choices about policy preferences instead of an opportunity to outwardly express one's beliefs in a community of like-minded peo-

---

[7]So named because Australian states in the 1850s were the first to use anonymous ballots for voting purposes.

ple. As the institution of voting became a more pure manifestation of democracy, the factors that motivated many voters were being stripped away. There was, as a result of progressive reforms, less response-ability. Voters were protected from any form of public scrutiny provided they did not willfully disclose their choice.

As the democratic values of individuality, rationality, and self-determination are institutionalized, an increasing amount of responsibility is passed from government and private institutions to the voter. Schudson (2000) explains that no European country has as many elections, offices, or jurisdictions as the United States. A voter in Chicago, for instance, is asked to choose among federal, statewide, county, and municipal candidates as well as elect judges and directors of agencies in unique jurisdictions like the Metropolitan Water Reclamation District of Greater Chicago. How is the average voter to be reasonably expected to know who is best fit to manage a major metropolitan water supply? With the increased number of offices in need of elected administrators, the voter is required to know a great deal in order to cast a vote she/he can consider reasonably justifiable. Party significance has been weakened as voting burdens increase. Criticizing this trend Patterson (1994) argues:

> The presidential election system places extraordinary demands on voters. . . . There was a time when America's policymakers understood that the voters should not be assigned this type of election decision, even if they were able to make it. Citizens are not Aristotles who fill their time studying politics. (p. 45)

Accompanied by social institutions, individuals were capable of reasoning socially. They may not have known about all the issues, but parties and unions were trusted to perform the function of equipping voters with the information necessary to justify their decisions. Though many have divested themselves from the parties, they still remain. Those *still* active, however, are different than they once were—less influenced by the middle and less response-able. Past party participation helped inform and limit choices and enabled individuals to shape policy and use their voice. When parties played a larger role, though the individual had less power, the nominee selections were ultimately a function of deliberation.

What follows in Chapter 5 is a more particular discussion about specific changes in public behavior. It does not necessarily follow that the success of science caused people to view voting differently. Traditions and conventions of public behavior and social responsibility were deeply ingrained in early modern society. However, something had to happen for these traditions to be displaced. The following chapter outlines three arguments explaining how this occurred. Generally, the application of a modern scientific perspective of voting as practiced by swing voters is distanciated from functioning from within a public sphere held together by Mumford's (1934) "tissue of beliefs." This tissue has deteriorated. It is maintained that the knowledge and conventions governing public behavior have been lost, replaced by an exclusive valuation of the individual and the private or intimate sphere.

5

PRIMACY OF THE PRIVATE SPHERE

[Dick] Cheney, serving in his role as president of the Senate, appeared in the chamber for a photo session. A chance meeting with Sen. Patrick J. Leahy (Vt.), the ranking Democrat on the Judiciary Committee, became an argument about Cheney's ties to Halliburton Co., an international energy services corporation, and President Bush's judicial nominees. The exchange ended when Cheney offered some crass advice. "Fuck yourself," said the man who is a heartbeat from the presidency.

Helen Dewar & Dana Milbank
Washington Post

THE DEVOLUTION OF THE PUBLIC SPHERE

While volunteering to help in an Illinois state house race in October 2000 in the near south suburbs of Chicago, an area characterized by swiftly shifting demographics due in part to whites fleeing the growing minority population to the immediate north, south, and west, I attended a meeting at which both Republican and Democratic candidates from several surrounding districts appealed to African-American community pastors for their endorsements. The memorable part of the evening was the words of the only African-American candidate running in the three races. Willie Jordan Jr., the Republican candidate for nearby District 30, explained, after everyone else had spoken, that he should get their endorsements because he was the only candidate qualified to "keep it real." He subsequently lost, as is typically the case for Republican candidates in this location.

Beyond being some sort of street vernacular, the notion of "keeping it real" seems to resonate with people today. Not just the language, but the idea seems to have struck a chord. Sizing up friends or potential partners, people talk about how "real" the other is. We tend toward the people who are "real" while avoiding those who are "fake." For instance, this applies well to politicians. In Florida, Governor Jeb Bush has experienced trouble because of his get-tough policies on illicit drug use in light of his own daughter's publicly documented uses of several illegal substances, arrests, and treatments. Consequently, he was accused by some of being an absent father, pursuing his career at the expense of the rearing of his children. The latter was problematic as it was viewed by some as contributing to his daughter's problems and it distinctly contrasted with the get-tough family values rhetoric of this Catholic conservative governor. Politically worse than being a hypocrite, however, was the fact that he was considered by some to be "fake."

Although these instances definitely warrant criticism because of the evident contradictions between his political rhetoric and his own successes or failings as a father, others instances of being a "fake" politician simply illustrate an effort on the part of the politician to present a mature or responsible public persona. Jeb's brother, President George W. Bush, had developed a persona in the media prior to the 2000 election as a fratboy prankster. The documentary *Journey's With George* (Pelosi, 2002) exposes Bush as a fun-loving guy, willing to joke with reporters whom he likely suspected to be writing unfavorable articles about him. His private disclosure to then vice-presidential candidate Dick Cheney that a certain *New York Times* reporter was an "asshole" revealed a candid moment that jibed with the persona propagated in the mass media.

The accusation by former New York governor Mario Cuomo, that Bush lacked "gravitas" probably contributed to the Bush campaign's desire to alter Bush's image. Concerned that voters would view him as a political lightweight, the Bush campaign made a concerted effort to tailor his image to help quell voter apprehensions. The tenor and style of his convention address revealed the new public Bush persona; he stopped rocking up on his toes, grinning, and giggling. Though some voters felt that the new Bush was somewhat stiff and "fake," his latenight press conference responding to drunk-driving revelations, caused many to conclude that he was still, in fact, "real."

Lucky for Bush, his opponent made it virtually impossible for criticisms about Bush being fake or phony to matter. Perceived by many as possessing almost too much gravitas, after some elements of the press characterized him as being groomed since birth for the presidency, Al Gore was desperate to display a convincing private persona. This concern could not have been any more evident than during the ostensibly extemporaneous kiss between himself and his wife Tipper at the Democratic National Convention. Coupled with his dressed-down earth tones, it was clear to many that he was trying, despite being perceived by some as too hard, to seem like a regular guy.

Implicit in these anecdotes is our cultural devaluation of public persona that accompanies the general depreciation of the public sphere by U.S. culture. Aided by press reports of questionable behavior contrary to officially presented persona, the issue of the separation of private and public life has often become one of morality, not privacy. Two personae, it is believed, may indicate a person who is duplicitous and less trustworthy. We do not trust two-faced people. A sense of the private intimate individual suggests to us authenticity. It is quite likely that more U.S. voters watched George W. Bush kiss and cry on *The Oprah Winfrey Show* in 2000 than saw his nomination speech: Displays on Oprah are more real. These "real" people are received as down-to-earth and unpretentious. As a governor, Howard Dean was the only outsider and, thus, the least *publicly* tainted candidate in the field of Democratic candidates for the presidential nomination in 2004. Coming from outside Washington, DC, he is perceived as not having been as influenced as the more seasoned U.S. senators and representatives. He seems more like us, more real. Had the press not framed his infamous yelp following his defeat in the Iowa caucuses as an episode of unbridled emotion, Dean might have had more of a chance at rebounding from the loss. Still, he follows in a tradition among political candidates who market themselves as down-to-earth real people—people outside the beltway. Minnesota Governor Jesse Ventura was one such candidate. Folksy billionaire Ross Perot was also perceived by many as the archetypically "real" candidate.

KEEPING IT REAL

> . . . confusion has arisen between public and intimate life; people are working out in terms of personal feelings public matters which properly can be dealt with only through codes of impersonal meaning.
>
> Sennett (1977)

What does Sennett (1977) mean in this quotation? He is arguing that the legitimacy and quality of public policy in a democracy depends on citizens functioning as public individuals. In *The Fall of Public Man*, Sennett explains that much of the sense of the public individual is lost. This idea of voters' perception of the public sphere being usurped by the standards of the private sphere, considered a superior and legitimate (natural) way of being, brings us to the first point in this chapter: the valuing of the private sphere relative to the public sphere discredits the public sphere as less natural. Public sphere behavior and discourse are no longer ruled by a set of shared "codes" or conventions. As mentioned above, politicians can be perceived as too formal and less real as a result. Thus, politicians find themselves in a sort of politician's double bind; they perform in a public sphere while attempting to appear as private individuals, all while avoiding the perception that they are duplicitous. President H. W. Bush, a child of considerable privilege, was well versed in the rules of public courtesy. His understanding of these codes were undoubtedly honed during his life of public service as the son of a U.S. representative, a soldier, diplomat, intelligence administrator, and vice-president. They were so well entrenched that his speech writer Peggy Noonan explained that Bush didn't even like to use personal or self-reflexive pronouns (2003). Nevertheless, he was discredited for exhibiting amazement at a grocery store UPC scanner, whereas audiences identified with President Clinton after he fielded a question on MTV about his underwear preference.

Why was Ross Perot's folksy discursive style so attractive to voters in 1992? Why does Tennessee Senator Lamar Alexander wear flannel shirts? Why does George W. Bush wear *Carhartt* jackets while visiting his ranch? Why have some presidential debates eschewed the podium for stools and utilized round stages? Why do presidential candidates now field questions from debate audience members instead of distinguished members of the press? Why was Bob Dole's wife employed so readily in his 1996 presidential campaign and praised for her ability to step down from the stage at the Republican National Convention to talk closely with the delegates? I maintain that the public sphere has been shaped by an increasingly deficient understanding of equality. Public conventions have been exchanged for an ethos revering freedom and self determination versus any type of conformity. Politicians are praised for reinventing everything from themselves, government, and politics. Necessity, invention's mother, is dead. Instead, invention seems to spring forth from the head of the god of novelty to tell us that all things new and different exceed the imperative of the status quo.

Stating that no rules at all have replaced traditional rules of public behavior, however, is too sweeping and I do not intend to paint with such a broad brush. In fact, there are rules, they are just camouflaged. This is true to the extent some people can be more real than others. In pop culture, it is extremely important for a celebrity to be perceived as real or "street." An extreme example is the deceased celebrity named Old Dirty Bastard (ODB). In addition to having thirteen children with various mothers (Ol' Dirty Bastard, 2003), he is accused of cashing welfare checks while his albums were soaring, he was arrested more than ten times and charged with drug possession, assault, and making terrorist threats, and he was only recently released from prison (Orlov, 2003). Though counterintuitive, his prison time and outrageous behavior operate as his street pedigree, verifying for others that he is genuine or real. This qualifies him to authoritatively rap as he does about matters of consumption and copulation. Meanwhile, celebrities who have avoided prison and have accrued wealth find the need to periodically remind us how real they are. In "Jenny from the Block" Jennifer Lopez sings that "everybody mad at the rocks that I wear." She dismisses these concerns, reminding her fans that "nothing phony with us, make the money, get the mansion, bring the homies wit us." She is, after all, still Jenny from the block.

There is little reason to believe that the same dynamics don't apply to presidential candidates. This is true to the extent that presidential candidates don't try to develop the persona of a "serious" or "experienced" candidate. The only headline made by a candidate refusing to appear on *The Oprah Winfrey Show* or *Late Night with David Letterman* will likely read that the candidate was out of touch. Refusal to participate on such programming was one criticism of George H. W. Bush (Dowd, 1992). On the other hand, senators, those most intimately involved in federal policy development, are rarely nominated by their parties to run for president (Wattenberg, 1991). None have been elected president since Johnson, who had the advantages of incumbency under unfortunate circumstances. Public policy wonks are not admired. As one subject interviewed put it, "Familiarity [of politicians] breeds contempt." She was only partly correct—public experience breeds contempt. Having ventured too long into the public sphere, politicians are perceived as having compromised their private authenticity for public successes. They talk in language rarely understood or appreciated.

Why does any of this matter to this particular study? The voters involved in this project barely mention any amount of public involvement, and rarely do they discuss issues with respect to their greater social value. These attitudes coupled with a general disdain for debate or deliberation indicates an ignorance about the conventions and functions of public involvement. Moreover, these voters were more concerned with voting or being right than they were with discussing the overall virtues of policy (presuming an ability to separate the two). In short, the extent of their public participation has been reduced to being nothing more than anonymous voters; they function almost exclusively as political consumers.

Fundamentally, what has caused this devaluing of and adherence to the public sphere's codes? The answer to this question lies in understanding the distinction between public and private spheres and the development of individualism in modern Western societies. In short, individualism has fundamentally altered how politics is "done." We are, as a cultural matter of practice, more individually involved. The ego is seen as less collectively constituted than it has been in the past, which means our inherent allegiances to others have been reduced. This is true to the extent that paying taxes and voting are, for some, the limits of one's public obligation. Given our rhetorical tendency to couple death with taxes, it is quite clear the *joy* with which we participate. The argument that this phenomenon is occurring is based centrally in Habermas' (1962/1989) distinction between the public and private spheres. It is argued that the public sphere was a cultural outgrowth that arose as was needed to distinguish itself from a more private sphere. The sphere of the home was one that developed in contradistinction to the state.

We first see this with the ancient Greeks. Greek society involved the notions of *polis* and *oikos* into their understanding of citizenship. The *polis* is the equivalent of the public. In it, politics was performed by all of those materially freed from the domestic or material environment of the *oikos*. What was significant for the Greek citizen was the freedom to participate in public decisions. This freedom was made possible by slaves and women who managed the domestic environment. The end sought by citizens was the ability to participate, not so much the nature of the decisions rendered by that participation (Pocock, 1995)

Admittedly, the practice of slave labor premised on the denial of human rights to some ethnicity, race, or state of indenture, as well as the subjugation of women through marriage were what enabled people (men) to invest their time in the public sphere. Pocock (1995) tells us about the nature of citizenship dilemmas with which many Western societies have found themselves faced.

> If one wants to make citizenship available to those to whom it has been denied on the grounds that they are too much involved in the world of things—in material, productive, domestic, or reproductive relationships—one has to choose between emancipating them from these relationships and denying that these relationships are negative components in the definition of citizenship. (p. 33)

Most Western democratic societies have chosen to deny that domestic preoccupation disqualifies one from participating as a citizen. As the feminist motto goes, "the personal is the political." Influenced by these attitudes, today's political practices are markedly different from the Greek notion of citizenship.

It should be of little surprise that voter participation was greater in the early days of the United States as opposed to today (excluding of course those denied the right to vote). The home space was managed by others. Propertied people had more resources that enabled them to follow public issues and governance. Today, however, nearly every citizen of the United States 18 years or older has been enfranchised. One exception includes felons, and efforts are being made by some in Congress to grant them the right to vote (Richey, 2002).

Our own notion of citizenship is modeled more on the Roman notion of the citizenship than the Greek. The Roman citizen possessed privileges as guaranteed by law. The term *republic* is derived from the Roman notion of *res publica*. *Res*, or "things" modifies *publica*. Whereas liberation from property one owned constituted Greek citizenship, the Roman notion of property simply became defined as that which was owned by citizens. "The citizen, redefined as a legal rather than a political being, found himself connected to a world of things which he possessed and rights to things which the law would also treat as his possessions" (Pocock, 1995; p. 41). Roman citizenship was a right as determined by law, not as determined by one's material conditions. The result of law, be it natural law or the law of a monarch, "decenters and may marginalize the assembly of citizens" (Pocock, 1995, p. 39). Codified as law, these ideas manifest today as our modern or rational attitude.

As indicated in Chapter 4, it was not until much later in United States history that more progressive notions supplanted the idea that land ownership qualified one as a citizen worthy of public participation. The problem for the United States is that this conceptualization of citizen, defined as such by law, is no longer inherently public or political. The attitude, faculties, and knowledge necessary to participate in governance have become lost as the public and private spheres, more distinct in the past are worse than conflated today. Instead, it seems, the public sphere is nearly lost, overcome instead by the dictates of the private sphere.

More than a discreet place the public sphere is simply evoked when people engage in discourse about matters pertaining to something more than the lives of ourselves and our intimates. In this respect, deliberation is de-liberating; it places limits on what can be said, who can say it, and how it can be said. Public concerns deal with all individuals of a society comprising not an aggregate but a community. There is a difference between functioning in the public, performing a public function, and reasoning about public concerns. One can perform private acts in public. We are reminded of this every time a person answers a cellphone in a movie theater. Private concerns, concerns of the self and those with whom we are most intimately tied, are both emulated by the behavior of the person as well as shared publicly. The talker talks as loudly as she can in order to satisfy her immediate needs. During the conversation, all manner of topics are discussed with seemingly little concern for the way strangers in her presence might react. There is no courtesy exhibited for the others inhabiting that public space.

Public functions can also be performed, but with a private concern in mind. Attending a Catholic high school outside Chicago, I was taught to perform service for others. Though told that service was necessary for reducing our stay in Purgatory, central to the instruction was reflection on how good service made us *feel*. We were asked to reflect, journal, and share verbally with others the good feeling of doing God's work. We were never taught that service was a civic or social responsibility. Instead we were taught that justification for such service was individually grounded as opposed to publicly grounded. Though the church might argue that service has the intended effect of evangelizing new Catholics, our religion teachers had more pragmatic concerns in trying to influence our behavior. They appealed to the individual.

Generally, the private sphere began as a place of freedom and protection from the domination of the state (Habermas, 1962/1989). The privacy that the ancient Greeks enjoyed was a freedom from tyranny or feudalism. The private sphere, complete with one's own private belongings, was controlled by the individual. From this sphere, the individual ventured into the public sphere to convene with and argue with others about the direction of the state. Many of these presuppositions carried over into modern Europe. Habermas writes, "The bourgeois public sphere may be conceived above all as the sphere of private people come together as a public" (p. 27). These private individuals in the public sphere relied upon reason—their ability to reason about the topics about which they were educated or involved. These people had property and to some extent were educated, thus they were aware of and familiar with the world of objects they subject to discussion (p. 37).

It was from this practice of public discourse and reason that the legitimation of state power and its laws was derived. Habermas (1962/1989) writes:

> A political consciousness developed in the public sphere of civil society which, in opposition to absolute sovereignty, articulated the concept of and demand for general and abstract laws and which ultimately came to assert itself (i.e., public opinion) as the only legitimate source of this law. (p. 54)

He argues that these people convened in the public sphere, and through discussion confirmed the perspectives and points of view of one another, perspectives believed to have emerged from their private more intimate (subjective) experiences. As noted, some scholars of the period believed that the conclusions drawn constituted truth; that through sufficient reflection, reason, and debate, one could surmise the "right" path for a society. Some scholars (e.g., Mill & Toqueville) believed differently, that public decisions were the product of prejudices and mere public opinion. These two positions mark differences between conservatives and liberals in U.S. democracy, respectively.

The latter position, however, is in no way a criticism of democratic practices; these writers are not characterizing democracy as subject to arbitrary dynamics. They do not advocate relativism. One should not take comfort in these philosophies when strictly pursuing ones' own personal interests in the public sphere. Voters, according to Mill and Toqueville, may not be tapping some transcendental truth when they vote or deliberate but public recourse to reason and deliberation are the best measures for determining the better actions to be taken by government. Deliberation allows citizens the opportunity to decide if policies are in the interests of the larger society, helps them to anticipate policy limitations or failure, and contributes to social transparency.

In any event, to the extent that legislation derived its legitimacy from discourse among a reasoned public, whether their conclusions constituted truth or not, this governing modality marked a significant improvement over more autocratic governing alternatives. However, when reasoned judgment is undermined, democratic governance experiences significant problems such as the ones noted in this project: the loss of social concern, deliberation, and community. Habermas (1962/1989) writes,

> In the course of our century, the bourgeois forms of sociability have found substitutes that have one tendency in common despite their regional and national diversity: abstinence from literary and political debate. On the new model the convivial discussion among individuals gave way to more or less noncommittal group activities. These too assumed fixed forms of informal sociability, yet they lacked that specific institutional power that had once ensured the interconnectedness of sociable contacts as the substratum of public communication—no public was formed around "group activities". (p. 163)

Putnam (2000), anticipated by Henry (1965) and Packard (1974), makes a very similar argument, explaining that individuals in the United States are, in large part, failing to engage each other in a face-to-face way. He marshals evidence indicating that "group participation" today largely consists of contributing money to those organizations. Even though the groups and organizations to which people belong are demanding less in terms of time and effort, per capita memberships have been experiencing steep declines. It seems little else is stepping in to replace the group's role as conduits for public participation. Why did people begin to engage less in the public sphere? Why is there a devalued perception of the value of this activity? Habermas suggests that leisure pursuits *replace* public activity, but he does not explain why; his work implies, however, that the availability of leisure time enabled people to disengage themselves from concerns of political necessities.

How do traditions of critical, literary, and deliberative activity find their way out of cultural practice? How is the cultural rationale constituting the foundation for such practices replaced, and what replaces it? Putnam (2000) argues that time demands, suburban sprawl, electronic entertainment, and participatory attrition among generations each contribute to the reduction of participation. Sennett (1977), however, proffers an explanation that helps us understand why our culture seems to have allowed civic engagement to be supplanted by the factors Putnam identifies. Sennett gives several answers to these questions in his attempt to explain why people have withdrawn from the public sphere—which is to say that they no longer act "publicly" in public. He uses the word *fall* to describe this *withdrawal*, which is more apt than withdrawal because the word better communicates the idea that people do not consciously opt out of public participation. Instead, contemporary culture and its conventions seem to offer little rationale for such activity and enable people to feel satisfied with their present levels of participation. He argues that we experience a "public life in which people behave, and manage their behavior, only through withdrawal, 'accommodation,' and 'appeasement'" (p. 36).

Dealing with similar constructs as Habermas (1962/1989), Sennett (1977) describes the public and private spheres as two components of a molecule, combining to constitute something new with unique properties of its own. Without these two components in balance with one another, the nature of their combined product is fundamentally altered for the worse. Upsetting the balance, he explains, were the characteristics of advanced capitalism and their resultant influences on the family, as well as ontological characteristics of the age with respect to secular concerns versus transcendent concerns.

With regard to family, Sennett (1977) maintains that capitalism's failings during the nineteenth century caused people to retreat into spheres where they were more likely to find stability or the ability to exert control.

> Using family relations as a standard, people perceived the public domain not as a set of social relations . . . but instead saw public life as morally inferior. Privacy and stability appeared to be united in the family; against this ideal order the legitimacy of the public order was thrown into question. (Sennett, p. 20)

In a "highly mobile, urban, class society" where there are fewer lasting ties among people in their immediate communities, it becomes less necessary to know well the people outside our tight intimate circles. Since the industrial and democratic revolutions, Schudson (1986) argues, we rely more on consumer signs and symbols to communicate our identity and status with others. Beyond our ability to size up the status of those we encounter in public, clothing and accessories enable us to know little else about the inhabitants of our lifeworld. Mumford (1989) explains:

> The town housewife, who half a century ago knew her butcher, her grocer, her dairyman, her various other local tradesmen, as individual persons, with histories and biographies that impinged on her own, in a daily interchange, now has the benefit of a single weekly expedition to an impersonal supermarket, where only by accident is she likely to encounter a neighbor. (p. 512)

Given the paucity of public engagement and the substitutes for it that our culture has developed, there is little mystery about why individuals have become less familiar with and/or appreciative of the conventions of public participation.

As culture increasingly exalted the "etiquette" of the private sphere, the understanding of the private sphere changed, as did the role of the public sphere in relation to it. In short, the public and private spheres were no longer considered necessary compliments of one another. Instead, the private sphere was considered a respite from the public. In the private sphere, the individual was considered safe when behaving naturally. The home life was one of natural behavior accompanied by looser clothing and looser talk. By virtue of its being more natural than the conventional public sphere, it came to be viewed as better. Its roots were grounded in nature, a lasting and permanent ontological base relative to the conventional and arbitrary public sphere. The private sphere was created *for* humans whereas the public sphere was created *by* humans. One retreated from the public sphere to exist in this more natural or healthy private environment. Liberated from the private sphere by property, wives, domestic servants, and slaves, ancient Greeks viewed entry into the public sphere as a privilege and necessity. The more contemporary modern individual finds refuge from the limiting conventions of the public sphere in the home.

During the seventeenth and eighteenth centuries, Sennett (1977) notes, bourgeois families began rejecting the practice of raising young children as adults, dressing them as adults, educating them as adults, and expecting them to behave as adults, in favor of allowing the children a more natural existence, allowing them to experience something termed "childhood." Considered a natural stage in life, it was increasingly believed that a child should not be denied his/her childhood. More generally, the natural or "self-evident" right to life, as found in the U.S. Declaration of Independence, involved more than the right to live. One's right to life meant that s/he should not be denied care and nurturance. People may not have been granted rights to income or healthcare by this, but equally revolutionary for the time were codified rights to equal treatment under the law and a presumption of dignity. Class distinctions were discredited because they were public conventions that limited the more natural self. Thus began the process of modifying social conventions when they "produced extremes of distress or pain" (Sennett, 1977; p. 98).

Habermas' (1962/1989) notion of courtesy involved the idea that one typically behaved according to social conventions in the public sphere out of respect for others. This term, *courtesy*, is a remnant from the days of European monarchies wherein one assumed a particular mode of behavior when communicating with the monarch or members of the court. To the extent that these conventions were upset by Western societies when they were considered harmful or limiting evidences the adaptability of these societies. The suffrage movement of the 1920s and the civil rights movement of the 1960s ultimately are good examples of this; our nation's willingness at times to accommodate civil disobedience is a very positive indication of our culture's willingness to disregard or amend stifling social conventions. Along with this willingness to alter the public domain, however, came an increasingly distrustful attitude toward the public sphere, which is made evident by the introduction of the idea of liberty and the consequent suspicion targeting the public situation.

Sennett (1977) argues that the idea of liberty is vague at best. How does one know when she *has* liberty or has *experienced* liberty? Liberty is experienced as a general liberation from social convention such that the individual personality may not be limited. As Western cultures increasingly celebrated the individual personality, the presumption grew that social convention was arbitrary and harmful to the unfettered and genuine realization of the personality. Sennett criticizes liberty as an abstracted notion exemplifying humanism sans social obligation. The individual's personality marked the triumph of natural human nature over the limitations of transitory and arbitrary conventions of human design. *Personality* has become a god-term. A person can aspire to become a personality. We exalt those credited with having personality, those who demonstrate and celebrate their freedom from the stifling limitations of conformity. Madonna and Roseanne Barr are personalities. I wouldn't argue that they aren't talented, but few will deny that their notoriety wasn't garnered by their outrageous behavior. In light of this assessment, it is little surprise that many in our culture would embrace Ross Perot and Jesse Ventura while looking upon Al Gore and John Kerry with suspicion.

Increasingly perceived by our culture with contempt, we lose our ability to function effectively within the public sphere. As such, we surrender it to others in favor of protecting and securing the intimate and immediate. Putnam (2000) explains that the costs of performing everyday life activities increases as public interaction decreases.

> As the social fabric of a community becomes more threadbare . . . its effectiveness in transmitting and sustaining reputations declines, and its power to undergird norms of honesty, generalized reciprocity, and thin trust is enfeebled. (p. 136)

This is a phenomenon that those living in urban areas know best. Individuals wishing to fully develop their personalities and fully be themselves, though tolerated, often find their differences underappreciated in a city forum where anonymity and atomism rule. Anonymity enables people in high density to function, regardless of their close proximity. Difference is tolerated because it is presumed; liberty is assured when everyone is ignored. This, however, is unsatisfying for the individual as his/her expressions go unrecognized and are taken for granted as part of the city motif. Although individuality is likely to be best appreciated among communities small enough to foster familiarity, the surveillance inherent to small communities can suppress and limit one's expressive freedom. Considering the value placed on the development and display of individual personalities by our culture, both types of community offer isolation either from others (as is the case with the city) or from self (as is the case with the small community).

Generally, political performance and outcomes are impacted by these cultural values and traditions; the individual withdraws from the public sphere altogether, not necessarily in pursuit of anonymity but in favor of safer and more natural havens in which s/he is appreciated. Families, circles of friends, work acquaintances, Internet groups, and chatrooms may fulfill these interpersonal needs. Among these groups, individuals can find recognition, and inasmuch as the group is interdependent, one is less likely to be rejected. Increasingly then, one's experiences are his/her own. The world is more subjectively rather than communally experienced. The individual decreasingly engages others publicly in a way that could provide ground for making public judgments. Sennett (1977) sums this point up well:

> ... the belief in direct human relations on an intimate scale has seduced us from converting our understanding of the realities of power into guides for our own political behavior. The result is that the forces of domination or inequity remain unchallenged. (p. 339)

In pursuit of the intimate sphere as the only genuine sphere, the public sphere is abandoned. We *consume* arguments but fail to participate by submitting our own. Other powers are at the wheel, and those included in this study passively nod with approval or disapproval failing to offer alternative routes.

POLITICAL COMMUNICATION CONSUMPTION

> The world fashioned by the mass media is a public sphere in appearance only.
> Habermas (1989/1962)

Paralleling and related to the cultural changes that have occurred in the public and private spheres is a transformation of our culture's use of information. Certainly, the public citizen needs to be informed about the issues that matter. The Greek citizen learned about these issues both by bringing his domestic experiences to the discussion— public service in the form of military participation—and interacting with others in the public sphere or the marketplace. Equipped with these, the Greek citizen was capable of participating knowledgeably. Much has changed, however, as information has been transformed into a commodity (mass). One either has it or does not have it. In an information society, the more you have, the better equipped you are. Today, it matters less what one critically does with that information. The time it takes a person to criticize information is time enough for more or contradictory information to come along. Our coping mechanism is a reliance or faith in the mythos of technocracy (Roszak, 1969).

This is the culture in which today's voters finds themselves—a culture characterized by chronic anxiety about new information. This is not an anxiety that some new information might come along but a presumption that too much is bound to. One has to have the latest news. Our pagers sound when new news is made available, but if waiting between beeps is too cumbersome, then one need only get an Internet-ready cell phone or Wi-Fi PDA to visit their favorite news Web page. No sooner do we get the news then there is new news to get. As a result, our culture has largely lost the capacity to process this news. The arts of public deliberation and criticism are dying at the same time as we have lost our ability to judge information due to both its quantity and the loss of judgmental ground.

> The tie between information and action has been severed. Information is now a commodity that can be bought and sold, or used as a form of entertainment, or worn like a garment to enhance one's status. It come indiscriminately, directed at no one in particular, disconnected from usefulness; we are glutted with information, drowning in information, have no control over it, don't know what to do with it. (Postman, 1990)

It is argued here that our modern relationship to information has made it more difficult to be public citizens. This is true for the following reasons. First, information is packaged in a way that discourages disagreement or criticism. Second, news is decontextualized; it is presented in a way that fails to make clear its relevance to the consumer. Third, there exists too much information with which voters can reasonably cope. Finally, information consumers have less publicly shared ground upon which to derive trust in their judgments.

Habermas (1962/1989) argues that information consumption is a precondition for successful democracy. What is implied by consumption here is quite simply that someone collects and produces information with the intention of exchanging it with some other party for another commodity. As public deterioration began to occur, less discussion (processing) took place about this information.

> In the course of our century [twentieth], the bourgeois forms of sociability have found substitutes that have no tendency in common despite their regional and national diversity: abstinence from literary and political debate. On the new model the convivial discussion among individuals gave way to more or less noncommittal group activities . . . —no public was formed around "group activities." (p. 163)

People did less with more; a system that relied on criticism and deliberation had begun to be powered solely by consumption.

Just as the elements of leisure became increasingly available to the lower classes, as people other than those of the propertied classes were enfranchised, both leisure items and information changed fundamentally. "To the degree that culture became a commodity not only in form but also in content, it was emptied of elements whose appreciation required a certain amount of training" (Habermas, 1962/1989, p. 166). Culture and information became consumption-ready. Although significant merit has been found in deconstructing cultural boundaries and mixing high-culture with low (I'm not elitist), dulling discourse to make it more marketable has its problems. It marks the difference between explaining one's intentions to protect Social Security contributions in a "lock-box" (language of Al Gore) or explaining that the Social Security contributions will be withheld from the Federal discretionary budget followed by a feasible description for such a plan. The nation's ability to reason well about issues such as these presupposes an ability on the part of the citizenry to understand them.

Debate, for example, has fallen victim to the process of simplifying information for audiences, an unfortunate development considering its necessity in a thriving democracy. Presidential debates have been dumbed down to a painfully short series of stump speeches. Only during more recent elections have the candidates agreed to experiment with the rigid debate format that precludes candidate interaction. Still, very little interaction between the candidates occurs—hardly a deliberative forum. Even questions from the media and voters are approved by the candidates well ahead of the debate. We've been given reason to believe the president's press conferences are scripted ("Show time in the East Room," 2003).[1] This would not be problematic if voters themselves were engaged with one another over matters of state. Unfortunately, most are given the impression that the necessities of debate and criticism are satisfied by our televisions' talking heads. Fox and CNN provide a number of programs that involve clashes between hosts and field experts. CNN gives us James Carville, Paul Begala, Tucker Carlson, and James Novak while Fox gives hosts Hannity and Colmes. *Talkback Live*, for example, was one such CNN show that included experts, audience members, telephone guests, and e-mail. The show was a chaotic mess constituting little more than democratic junk-food: the consumer could fill up yet walk away with no cognitive nutrition. Habermas terms the intake of such material "a tranquilizing substitute for action" (p. 164). Putnam (2000) speculates that spectator aspect of all this devalues the face-to-face interaction necessary for democratic politics to operate.

> Without such face-to-face interaction, without immediate feedback, without being forced to examine our opinions under the light of other citizen's scrutiny, we find it easier to hawk quick fixes and to demonize anyone who disagrees. Anonymity is fundamentally anathema to deliberation. (p. 342)

---

[1] This piece documents President Bush's comment during a 2003 press conference revealing that the press-conference questions and reporter-selection order had been prescripted. He jokes with a CNN White House correspondent for asking permission to ask a question that had already been pre-approved.

This, he laments, does not happen because mediated deliberation is mistaken for the real thing.

Additionally, it is found that news is often presented as fact—undebatable. There is little debate to be had. As Habermas (1962/1989) points out, the early penny press sacrificed editorial and political discussion for sales. In the news there is an implicit denial about the existence of multiple points of view. The news, he puts it, appears "predigested." Today, sales govern how the news is produced. Debate and sociological analysis are generally avoided as they have less immediate audience appeal. A recent example of this lies in the story of the former NBC news anchor from Chicago, Carol Marin. Ms. Marin left as anchor of NBC's Chicago affiliate after the network made the decision to air commentary by Jerry Springer during the evening news. She left for Chicago's CBS affiliate with her credibility soaring, which allowed her to revamp the evening news in order to style it as more serious and legitimate. She decided to lend more air time to discussion and in-depth reporting, while cutting back on graphics, intimate-seeming banter, and promotions. Ultimately, the format failed because it did not improve audience share (Feder, 2001). She was then promoted to *60 Minutes II* as a correspondent, only to be replaced soon after by the more attractive Lara Logan (Feder, 2002).

There is also a careful distinction between the types of news offered that plays an important role here. Habermas's (1962/1989) language is interesting, referring to news as either "delayed reward news" or "immediate reward news." The distinction is clear; one derives an immediate reward from news that is arresting, that stops us in our tracks. Studying sociological themes, however, garners less immediate interest. Iyenger (1990) addresses a phenomenon quite similar, drawing a distinction between "episodic" and "thematic" news. He writes, "Television news, for instance, is an inherently 'episodic' or event-oriented medium: Televised news reports focus on concrete acts or 'live' events at the expense of general contextual material" (p. 21). Thematic news, on the other hand, examines phenomena as the product of long-term sociological dynamics. The latter type of reporting is often rejected for the former because episodic news is more interesting. We would much rather watch a poor family eat dog food than watch a reporter speculate about why this sort of thing happens. When poverty becomes a salient problem in the news, the description of the family's plight is inherently more interesting and more accessible to viewers than a discussion of sociological trends and debates about proposed causes. Framing news and issues in an episodic fashion contributes to its decontextualization. Stories about murder, muggings, and theft are ordered into discrete reports followed by stories about tax cuts. Presented this way, few will realize the link between them. Failing to understand the circumstances contributing to the story being covered, the consumer is ill-equipped to attribute blame. Poverty appears to just occur cropping up out of circumstances unique to the individual featured in the story. Iyengar (1990) notes that the result of this form of news coverage is that the viewer tends to blame the featured individual or family for their own circumstances; "They eat dog food because they are lazy."

Second, it is argued that the matters above coupled with the shear volume of information available to consumers politically anesthetizes people. Not only is much of the information encountered irrelevant to the individual's daily life, but its shear volume causes consumers to fundamentally alter how this information is consumed. The volume of information encountered by voters today has two serious impacts on a person's capacity to make election decisions. Postman (1986) explains that the decontextualization of news is partly a product of the types of media used to disseminate it. Only relatively recently have middle, working, and lower class people been able to access daily news from Texas, Hollywood, Ankara, Beijing, West Bank, and Baghdad. The advent of electronic media has expanded the world of the individual from the local to the universal. Telegraphy, he argues, initially allowed information to be broadly cast from its origin to its destination many states away. The result is that the consumer came to learn of happenings that mattered little to her/his daily life. ". . . the situation created by telegraphy, and then exacerbated by later technologies, made the relationship between information and action both abstract and remote" (p. 68). What is one to do with the information they receive today? Of what use is knowledge related to the value of Jennifer Lopez' engagement ring, Carnie Wilson's weight loss, or 10-car pile-ups in Milwaukee? Moreover, how can actual important information be made politically meaningful without contextualization? It is easy for me to know that information about the Lopez and Affleck engagement and break-up is worthless, however, what do I do with information about social problems like poverty? How can a voter reason that s/he should vote on an aspect of foreign policy when areas of the world such as Afghanistan only make the news when something of "episodic" significance occurs? The harm results from the fact that the viewer is rarely equipped to make relevant meaning of this abstracted information. If a bomb blows up in Afghanistan, why does that matter to the viewer? The images are gripping, but the relevance is lost. The context goes unexplained as the story is displaced by tomorrow's events elsewhere. Even for local matters about which voters are best equipped to make meaning (such as tax measures, water costs, job availability, and other matters that affect them directly) local information is a scarce commodity. Even if local news were more readily available, it would have a hard time competing with the more gripping episodic events like visually engaging reports of explosions, wars, fights, and car wrecks that occur worldwide on a daily basis.

Besides the decontextualized information that the media brings into our homes, Postman (1990) explains that so much information is produced and disseminated that consumers lose their ability to manage it.

> There is almost no fact—whether actual or imagined—that will surprise
> us for very long, since we have no comprehensive and consistent picture
> of the world which would make the fact appear as an unacceptable con-
> tradiction. We believe because there is no reason not to believe. No
> social, political, historical, metaphysical, logical or spiritual reason. We
> live in a world that, for the most part, makes no sense to us. Not even
> technical sense.[2]

He blames media for overwhelming people with information. With immeasurable quantities of information both produced, broadcast, and often contradicted each day, consumers lose the ground upon which to judge, make sense of or an orderly whole of information in their world. Without this ground, the ability to make decisions becomes increasingly difficult.

With so much information coming at us, in a sense, Postman (1986) claims that people stop trying to be critical consumers of information. I have heard my mother state, "Smoking may be bad for me, but I'm sure that if I wait a few days some study will tell me that cigarettes prevent heart attacks." Her comment is indicative of a dismissive coping mechanism wherein people find justification for spurning warnings in the perceived sea of warnings, studies, and facts disseminated by the mass media each day. There is no solid ground in a world filled with informational fissures and eruptions. One of the first to make a similar sociological argument, Henry (1965) adds:

> A phenomenon that is important to an understanding of our culture and,
> indeed, of the contemporary world is the underlying assumption of the
> modern world that one does not really know what one thinks one knows;
> that it is likely, on close investigations, to turn out to be wrong. This
> assumption of probably error inherent in all decisions helps create a con-
> dition of uncertainty, so that the torment of always being possibly wrong,
> or at least of not having the "best" answer to any of life's problems,
> becomes a dominating characteristic of modern life. (p. 15)

This applies to voters as well. What one knows, or thinks s/he knows, is constantly being upset. The cynical voter described by Hart (1999) exhibits disregard for new information, not because of a need to feel clever, but in order to stabilize his/her world. Pretending that one knows enough about politics is a way to make believe that there is a world out there about which people agree. Though one may empathize with this way of waring, ultimately it is a threat to reasoned democratic practice. It undermines reason and promotes indifference toward information potentially relevant to both the self and the other. Postman (1986) states, " . . . we are losing our sense of what it means to be well informed" (p. 107). Those who attend to the news may feel informed

---

[2]Taken from a speech delivered by Neil Postman titled *Informing Ourselves to Death*. Retrieved from world.std.com on September 16, 2002.

because they have acquired information, albeit of dubious quality. Others, as protection against the wave of data, pretend to be informed when they are not.

Finally, it is argued that being informed is a difficult task, relative to the efforts of those from previous generations because previous generations shared more assumptions upon which judgments rested. The reason for this is that there is less public engagement[3] and, as a result, less common ground upon which to render judgment about what constitutes sound information. Public engagement is a safeguard against anomie. When perspectivism and individualism elevated the ego to the point that the authority of religion and monarchial government were challenged, it became necessary for persons challenging those forms of authority to engage one another—to subject their views and understandings to intersubjective appraisal. Unfortunately, the forums and conventions for performing this appraisal are barely hanging on. Thus, little is challenged at all. ". . . in a world without spiritual or intellectual order, nothing is unbelievable; nothing is predictable, and therefore, nothing comes as a particular surprise" (Postman, 1990). As is seen in this study, those interviewed sought information yet offered little criticism. They were passive consumers. Though they received information promoting both candidates, they were rendered incapable of executing judgment over that information because they had no ground.

TIME POVERTY

The final explanation provided in this section is the argument that people simply do not have the time for public participation. This applies to nearly all political participants—swing voters, partisans, or nonvoters alike, though it is made apparent in the perceived limitations experienced by those interviewed. The demands placed upon contemporary U.S. lifestyles are excessive. In light of what is demanded of a person or family to survive in today's United States, it is quite easily argued that the demands placed on modern life far exceed the amount of time a person has available to become a well reasoned, critical, and publicly active individual unless they make such work a profession. As previously mentioned, the political demands alone are rather extensive (Schudson, 2000).

The United States' work habits have been shaped by the protestant work ethic, the modern notion of efficiency, and our consumerist culture. On the one hand, members of this culture are generally taught to be selfless, to measure their worth according to external or objective standards rather than internal or subjective standards. One's worth, then, is determined by the amount of work performed. According to this standard, someone who works more is of greater value than someone who works less. On the other hand,

---

[3]Putnam (2000) marshals a great deal of evidence supporting this claim.

the culture of the United States perceives the amount of outcome produced as also extremely important to determining worth. Enabled by the advent of the clock, the notion of efficiency or the amount produced for the time used, laborers and employers were provided with a way by which to measure the relative production of individuals over time.

Clues to this mentality can be found throughout the culture. For example, workers in the United States enjoy recreation during their time away from work, wherein one re-creates him/herself. Once re-created, a person is able to return more refreshed to work—though the amount of time used for recreation in the United States has been steadily falling (Schor, 1991). Another example involves the experience of women in the United States in their attempts to achieve a state of equality with men. For many, this has meant the freedom to determine for themselves their career paths without concern for traditions and conventions. This route provides clear standards for measuring performance and success relative to their male counterparts in terms of sales, salary, and promotion. As parity between men and women is more closely approached, it will undoubtedly be measured, in part, in economic terms. It will not be measured, however, by comparing relative time spent in the home. Ironically, the home is not considered a place of real work; this is reserved for the technical sphere. Few people are clamoring for men to spend more time in the home to help balance out the relative sex distribution in the workplace. If one is successful, generally it is in terms of work in the labor market. Today, both sexes seek daily to vacate their homes in their bedroom communities for the workplace where their value can be objectively determined in dollars and cents.

This ethic is reflected in the performance of U.S. labor. According to the Organization for Economic Cooperation and Development, the average worker in the United States spends 1,976 hours a year on the job while workers in most Western European countries work far fewer hours. The British work 10% less while Germans work 22% less than their counterparts in the United States. Additionally, a smaller percentage of people in these European countries work (Ferguson, 2003). Authors interviewing the French about their government-imposed 35-hour work week responded to their questions by explaining that the French have it right; "The economy is supposed to work for us, not the other way around!" (Nadeau & Barlow, 2003, p. 9). This comment, albeit anecdotal, combined with the institutionally shortened work week certainly reflects an attitude that stands in stark contrast to that of the United States in which $21 billion in unused vacation days is returned to employers each year ("Time Away," 2003). In contrast to a less work-anxious Europe, it is the culture of the United States that responded to Kellogg's shortened 32 hour work week (which subsequently resulted in increased worker efficiency) with statements like "only an idiot would think you can get as much working less instead of more hours a week" (Levine, 1997, p. 142).

This is our culture's attitude. The result is, according to Juliet Schor (1991), that since the 1940s the United States has been on a "trajectory of declining leisure" (p. 2). Compared with Germany and France, United States manufacturing employees work 320 more hours per year. This is the equivalent of two months work. U.S. fathers are working longer days into the evenings and more often working on weekends to extend hours or to take second jobs (p. 21). Moreover, in 1990, two-thirds of "married American women were participating" in the workforce (p. 25), a higher proportion than is found in any other country. Schor estimates that U.S. women work between 70 to 80 weekly hours combined on matters of employment, child care, and housework (p. 21). At the same time, however, hours worked in the home have shown little signs of change. Despite all the "time-saving devices" home labor requirements show little signs of decline. Though men are sharing more of the duties in the married household, the overall estimated numbers of hours worked in the home have remained the same since the 1960s (p. 35). Schor sites research showing that since 1973 free time, in terms of hours, has fallen about 40% from 26 weekly hours to 17 hours (p. 22). Hochschild (1997) notes that there appears to be little anxiety of returning to home and family as few people express a desire to work fewer hours. "The idea of more time for family life seems to have died, gone to heaven" (p. 27).

If people have little time at home and exhibit little desire to increase what news is available to them, it seems unlikely that voters are going to find *more* time to involve themselves with public concerns. As such, it is unlikely that a renewed sense of public concern will develop under the present cultural circumstances. Undoubtedly, people spend time both in the workplace and home discussing politics, but they are rarely engaged in a *public* way. Work in the private sector (technical sphere) and time in the home (private sphere) both involve private interests. As we race between the two, the public simply becomes space to be overcome quickly.

6

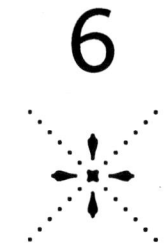

ALTERITY AS NECESSITY

> Selfishness blights the germ of all virtue; individualism, at first, only saps the virtues of public life; but in the long run it attacks and destroys all others and is at length absorbed in downright selfishness.
> De Tocqueville (1994)

The swing voters encountered in this study were found to be concerned enough to vote. They pay attention to politics to the extent they believe time permits. They eschew party affiliations that might unduly influence them, and they strive to be fair, all in keeping with the belief that biases (defined as a preference) are bad. Preparing to vote means accruing information while withholding judgment. Both major party candidates in the presidential race are given consideration because, in their view, doing anything less would be unfair to the candidate and, perhaps, the society. In sum, these characteristics describe an objective or scientific voting modality termed here the "modern swing voting ethic." The detachment distinctive of this voting modality shares a great deal with general dissociative trends found throughout contemporary society where silence between neighbors is the hallmark of being a good neighbor and public disengagement is positively coded as minding one's own business. We interpret our dissociation rationally to avoid implicating ourselves; this seems to be true of swing voters as well. In this chapter, I argue that social disengagement is inherently irrational, characterized by the pursuit of a collective magic/mythic consciousness. Participation is abandoned, forfeiting knowledge of self and other while relinquishing power to voices unlike our own—the more extreme. This chapter seeks to challenge the reader to reconsider the ontological assumptions that have brought our culture to this point, to bring them to awareness, and to subject them to criticism.

CONTEMPORARY SELF-UNDERSTANDING

Central to the arguments in this chapter is the idea that the result of public engagement is an understanding of the self vis-à-vis others and their needs. A public sense of self is necessary to develop ideas and balance the interests between self and others—that is, democratic necessities and justice. The objective/empirical ethic, however, fails to value or foster a publicly participative lifestyle. Democracy necessitates our willingness to endure the risks involved with participation, communication, encounters, engagement, and face-to-face exploration. Instead, we find today that many voters endeavor to be passive bystanders, similar to the way a jury remains quiet during courtroom argument. As such, citizens are immersed in an information environment wherein they are ill-equipped to make sound judgments about themselves, others, and society at large.

On its face, it may seem that there are two contradictory arguments here. On the one hand, I have maintained that voters are more individualistic while also arguing on the other hand that they have trouble expressing their own voice and participating in the public sphere. It stands to reason that highly self-involved individuals would have well-developed senses of themselves and their needs. My claim is better understood, however, if the reader recognizes the difference between the private and public individual. The individualistic contemporary is less familiar with his/her public self. His/her needs are not understood vis-à-vis the public, are not translated into public discourse, and are developed in an insular psychic environment. The reader won't find the argument here that individualistic voters do not know themselves well enough to know their own opinions. Instead, this is *all* they know. They know self to the exclusion of the other so as to be ignorant of the other. Relatedly, they know less of themselves as perceived by others. Lost in our public sphere is the practice of discourse performed for the purposes of exploring the needs of neighbors, strangers, and the greater whole. Putnam (2000) states, "Regular connections with my fellow citizens don't *ensure* that I will be able to put myself in their shoes, but social isolation virtually guarantees that I will not" (p. 340). Concomitant with the lack of familiarity with others is a prejudice toward doubt and skepticism concerning any form of ground upon which public judgments and decisions can be based. Replacing reason and judgment is a seeming confidence in a mythic understanding of democracy perceived to be so well-tuned that it requires little help from the busy work-a-day swing voter. So long as democracy is in place, the myth holds, society will inevitably progress most efficiently toward its object, without the interference of citizens—a teleology of progress. This modern voting perspective precludes the involvement of the seemingly well-developed modern individual in directing the ship of state. The swing voters' inhibitions are a product of what I term an "election scientist" model; these voters are content simply to study the issues at a distance and cast a vote, effectively divorcing themselves from the debate.

The following arguments are ontological; they assess the ontological presuppositions of contemporary culture in light of postmodern alternatives. Our contemporary culture generally places emphasis upon concrete and measurable production, external uniform notions of value, and efficiency. In part because of this ontological milieu, this modern voting modality exists and is perpetuated by its ability to adequately render sensibility to the lifeworld. Those guided by these unexamined attitudes or presuppositions may find it more difficult to accept them as antecedents to the consequences outlined here. The mode of public withdrawal discussed in this book presents problems both to the withdrawing individual and to society. For instance, if the reader accepts the notion that different experiences make us more broad-minded or cosmopolitan individuals, then it follows that failures to engage other people, in matters of either public or private concern, isolate us from the knowledge or the perspectives gained by engaging them. I can imagine readers incredulously asking, "So, I'm supposed to talk to the homeless man on the way to the train?" or some such question. Misgivings of this sort reflect the ontological presuppositions noted above. Conversations of this kind produce little if any concrete or measurable outcomes that fit any external notion of value. Because time is money, as our culture's reasoning goes, it is probably best saved rather than wasted on conversation with street people or others of ostensibly limited value. Our unexamined attitudes about efficiency often leave us with a lack of time for the types of engagement necessary for strong community. Mumford (1989) argues that though our civilization trumpets its successes in leaving behind medieval beliefs and traditionalisms for those of the Renaissance, medieval people had more time for conversation and community. They chatted and their chatting did not constitute wasted time. Hall (1990) identifies modern Western culture as the only one capable of understanding the concept of "doing nothing" because of our values of urgency and production. Regardless of innate human needs for social interaction, engagement with others has been redefined by our modern predilections for productivity as wasteful. The answer to the aforementioned question is not necessarily to discuss more but to be more aware of our attitudes and the modern demands on life that discourage discursive encounters.

Our failure to engage each other promotes a presumption of attitudinal uniformity and indifference; at least this appeared to be true for the people I talked to in this project. We either expect others to fit into the system or are indifferent toward those who don't, provided the offenders don't upset society's calm redundancy. The system's predictability and repetition fosters tranquility and serenity. Those embedded in this milieu lose themselves; others become like the many trees passed on the expressway—forgettable objects decorating or obstructing our path. The fruits of rational and industrial society, as perceived and pursued today, are various modes of disengagement (in effect, the ir-rational). Ironically, Gebser (1949/1985) describes the achievement of mental/rational consciousness (modernity) as the result of the ego emerging from the collective, an awakening of sorts. Modern societies are characterized by heightened awareness of self and world—the capacity and willingness to reflect on our individual lives in the world. Today, however, much of our culture is sounding a retreat, regressing to the safety of a prerational or mythical/magical awareness that constitutes "everything . . . of equal significance or validity" (p. 50): Equality! Why engage difference if everything is presumed equal? Without engagement, the self just exists, biding time at work and in the home pursuing interests that evidence its successes. Gilding one's cage by acquiring homes, automobiles, boats, or other possessions marking one's success may help an individual feel that s/he has realized the American Dream. Self- actualization for some has come to mean, in reality, the self merging with the collective dream. As such, the self aspires to Sameness.[1] Without the necessary resources for the conspicuous consumption just described, others opt to "check out," a voluntary retardation of waring into a consciousness that is predominantly magical. Some achieve this through the use of televisual entertainment (c.f., Fowles, 1992), sex, alcohol, or illicit substances (c.f., Morris, 1996). Lost in this consumptive escape (the contemporary model of successful being) is a self whose horizons are impregnated by interactions with others and their inherent difference, uniqueness, and potential—alterity. Individuals fail to acquaint themselves with other people in their environment. These concerns, however, are subsumed by a much larger failure by individual citizens to possess or exhibit concern for community and those constituting it. This leaves us with the justifiable impression of a diminishing concern for community and justice.

This argument is not to be confused with elitist criticism of bourgeois consumerist tastes. I'd have no place making such an argument, as my own admittedly questionable taste is not above reproach. Instead, this is calling into question the mode of marketed consciousness that accompanies both

---

[1]Same and Other are capitalized when used as Levinas did in his works. the Same is the generally perceived group. those who fit it, adapt, and aspire to be the same—to blend in. The Other is Levinas's notion of the astounding other whom we engage out of obligation, as opposed to the modern other who coexists with us and crosses our path.

consumption and democracy in our culture. Consumer status is foundational to the American Dream, and awareness of consumption's detrimental impact awakens us, disrupting what is mythologized by Madison Avenue experts as an enviable and comfortable existence. Often, we prefer not to acknowledge that our fertilizers harm the water supply, that our fossil fuels contribute to global warming, or that our water consumption dangerously taxes rivers and delicate habitats. The dissemination of such messages is popularly attributed to liberal media *bias*. How can one reasonably achieve the American Dream if s/he has to be worried about its ecological impact? By extension, disengagement from others also helps us maintain an avoidant and dreamlike existence. Note that the narrative of the American Dream, to the extent we can deduce one, doesn't involve/include others. The dream is fulfilled to the extent that one exceeds the material wealth of his/her parents and not as a result of knowing or helping the neighbors. Society's responsibility is to ensure the *right* to fulfill the dream. Social problems, made evident by means of engagement and dialogue, are rendered invisible by the totalizing ethos of equality that renders all things, people and ideas, equi-valent. Failure to listen to others, to respond, stifles the originary obligation that establishes my subjectivity to act on the Other's behalf. The isolated individual is not called into question by the Other and avoids both immediacy and the particularity of the unique need of the Other for social change or justice. The disengagement described is an oblique endorsement of the status quo— the smooth running system of U.S. democracy. The status quo is easier to endorse if I know less about whom it affects and how.

THE VALUE OF ALTERITY

The following argument provides an explication of the claims already made and of the implications that follow. In short, it is maintained that discursive encounters with other people are necessary for democracy to function well, so long as its performance is assessed according to its responsiveness to citizen needs. The voters analyzed in this study come closer than they realize to the voter ideal, the scientific voting model, to which they aspire. Generally, this ideal values disengagement. This ideal is constituted, according to swing voters, as public distance, thoughtfulness, and reflection; the swing voter loads each of these with positive valences. It is doubtful, however, that the habits of participation documented here are the products of reflection. Instead, the greater phenomenon of disengagement, I suspect, evidences something more significant. Swing voters along with the more disaffected nonvoters manifest a larger trend favoring public disengagement altogether. This is more of a cultural *attitude* as opposed to a choice. Those disengaging do not necessarily reason that "dropping out" is best, but in the present context it *seems* like the thing to do. Social disengagement is troublesome for democracy, however, for two reasons: First, the concerns of many may not be encountered by others; second, those same concerns may also never be formulated or considered by the individuals in the first place sans public engagement.

The prevalence of this attitude has developed relatively recently in history. Habermas (1962/1989) argues that letter writing constituted one of the most important developments in Western society with respect to the development of modern democracy. It was through writing, he maintained, that people came to view themselves and their thoughts in light of others' (the public's) scrutiny. Their ideas, developed in writing, were developed *for* an audience *with* the audience in mind. Ideas, once present in the mind of the narcissistic modern individual, were realized in writing and submitted to others for their edification, enjoyment, and stimulation. Bourgeois letter writers, he explained, "formed the public sphere of a rational-critical debate in the world of letters within which the subjectivity originating in the interiority of the conjugal family, by communicating with itself, attained clarity about itself" (p. 51). What is important here is not so much that the political participants of the 17th and 18th centuries wrote about themselves, but that they wrote letters in a style intended for the consumption of others. Happenings, thoughts, and ideas were written in a style and manner that befitted public exposition. In putting thought to paper for a general audience, the writer's thoughts became intelligible to a more generalized reader. Thoughts were formulated in light of their anticipated reception by another. In the process, the writer became more aware of his/her own attitudes as well as concerned for those of his/her reader. Additionally, the reader was exposed to the ideas of the writer.

Among other things, this development in writing helped constitute a public way of thinking wherein ideas were realized on paper and adapted for a larger audience in the process. This form of discourse was designed for the purpose of encountering others. It has been argued here that people today exhibit private behavior in a "public" space with little concern for convention, courtesy, or concern for the other. Coupled with this is a lesser developed sense of self as a publicly engaged entity. One's own ideas are less often entertained and developed by the self through the process of preparing and sharing those ideas with others. Mass mediated information consumption has supplanted reflection and refinement of thought for public consumption or debate. Occupied by the reception of mass-mediated messages, people become less familiar with what is on their own minds. Ideas emerge/evolve more externally than internally; ideas are provided prepackaged rather than arising in the intersubjective exposure and exchange with others which is creativity's font. We entertain fewer thoughts altogether—an argument that proceeds from the presumption that people who don't engage publicly reflect differently about themselves in the world.

If today the private and the public spheres have become confused or conflated, what are the harms? If you, the reader, buy the argument posited in this book, then what are you to think? After all, individuals have been freed from stultifying conventions to express themselves more freely, right? A recent caller to a talk radio show in central Florida commenting on dress codes remarked that during his high school years in the 1960s all the kids dressed similarly without being compelled to; fewer cliques existed so people conformed as a standard more broadly held. Today, however, his impression is that the many freedoms his children are afforded enable them to be happier because they will be able to "find themselves" earlier. This man's talk evidences our culture's valuing of individualism and celebration of the self's uniqueness and our presumption that these freedoms, as they manifest today, mark our progress in the liberation of the human being. Withering adherence to seemingly arbitrary rules of public courtesy and the consequent public displays of uniqueness and self have convinced us that we have more freedom.

To what end do people in our society attain the individual freedoms described? Certainly, this is a question to be answered individually. In short, the answer could be "To whatever end I want!" More and more, it seems the net benefit is gained in fuller expression of the self, a more completely realized ME! Implicit in the contemporary anxiety about being one's self, not selling out, and keeping it real, is that there is such a thing as a pure, true, and static ego upon which is imposed convention and constraint. The progressive notion that the self isn't static, that it is vulnerable to others in a broad intersubjectivity, and that the self can be called into question (willed to change) counter to a mass-mediated status quo is absent from this perspective. Today one's position seems more likely to be uncovered, not created; teleologically, the self values fulfillment and completion not discovery and invention—the latter being the true humanistic objective of liberty. Though generally accepted as arising from an innate sense of compassion, kindness toward others in private and public spheres is thwarted; entailments of the notion of ego seeking full manifestation imply that bonds or responsibilities between people are of secondary concern. Each person constitutes an atom that longs to be both free from others and to also be self-actualized. This value hierarchy promotes a self-serving indifference toward others. The good individual, according to this standpoint, is defined as the one who is not in the other's way, "just doing my own thing" as it's said. Just as Sennett (1977) explained that "public" is a name given to space to be overcome, people too are obstacles to be surpassed or managed. If I can best predict and control the behaviors of those with whom I cohabit the community, I can most efficiently accomplish my goals. Others, like space, must be surmounted.

Others are those around whom we navigate toward the fuller realization of our nascent selves. As such, the individual is isolated from the greater whole. Community as a result becomes aggregate, and the rules of individualism govern both private and public spheres. Among many of the obvious harms to the self—loneliness, isolation, and anomie—that which is central to this book are individualism's impact on vigorous democratic practice. A society that celebrates equality and its entailments (an abstraction of the first order) to the extent that ours does ultimately undermines the possibility of encounters with and recognition of difference. Our culture's notion of equality functions to quiet discourse in two ways: on the one hand, equality assumes that all people are the same (equality subsumes difference).

> Democracy presumes a universe of interchangeable, equal units that have no inherent qualities of differentiation. In most cultures "equality" is a farfetched idea that is not supported by experience. People within the group manifest different qualities, not e-quality. (Kramer, 1997, p. xiv)

The notion that all are Same facilitates disengagement because there is nothing to be gained by engaging those who are *not* myself; from this vantage point we are all Same. Forfeited is the valuing of difference and a corresponding attentiveness encouraging exchange of knowledge, beliefs, and perspectives. On the other hand, equality ensures the courtesy of *tolerating* difference when it is found. This is quite likely the reason many younger college-educated adults migrate disproportionately toward cities (Franklin, 2003); they value the city because the ideal of respect and tolerance is perceived to be more completely realized, supporting a lifestyle deemed more cosmopolitan and liberated. The first two rules of city life learned by urban transplants further evidences Sennett's (1977) argument; city-goers must appear indifferent to their surroundings and never make eye contact. Nothing will attract solicitations for contributions from street residents faster than a person acting as though s/he hasn't seen the buildings there a thousand times before. Look down and look away from both the buildings *and* the people. People in such a culture are tolerant of difference provided you don't engage them with it. Cultures valuing equality must take care to avoid confusing tolerance with ignorance that voids human diversity.

RE-EXAMINING CONTEMPORARY ONTOLOGY VIS-À-VIS CIVICS

Many facets of modern ontology implicit in what has already been described are facing a crisis of confidence. The currents of consciousness that propel us through our lifeworld are increasingly being resisted because of a more acute awareness of their inability to resolve many of the problems our culture now faces. The presumptions of a monolithic knowledge and the independence of the individual have been unreflectively taken to a point of absurdity, manifest throughout our lives in myriad ways that are no longer beneficial. Our culture can respond in one of two ways to the inadequacies of modernism. Modernism could further entrench itself, blaming its failures on our lack of rigorous adherence. That is, it could more strictly cleave the dictates of our present cult of liberty and individualism. Modernism, on the other hand, could become something that is as yet rarely conceived by turning the scrutiny of modern consciousness in its own direction to reveal its limitations among its strengths. From such scrutiny are harvested the fruits of phenomenology, an integral ontological knowledge incorporating the necessity of human liberty *and* the obligation to Other.

Husserl's (1954/1970) phenomenological project is notable for highlighting the ontological confusion promoted by different schools of thought in the academy. Considering himself a positivist, his goals were not to question or criticize ontology. Instead, he sought to unify academic knowledge in a way that reconciled competing notions of reality. Abandoning or bracketing presuppositions about the nature of reality, whether psychological, biological, geological, historical, or physical, he hoped to resolve these differences by directing our attention to the "things themselves"—the contents of the human lifeworld. The lifeworld, he argued, was synthesized or intended by consciousness. By analyzing the contents of consciousness we could peel away the contingent and sedimented layers of meaning in order to most accurately understand how the world presents itself to consciousness. Phenomenology's purpose is, according to Husserl, to better understand pure consciousness—the transcendental ego—and how the world is perceived without contingent influences. Those who followed in the tradition balked at this notion, arguing instead that the phenomenologist could not extrude consciousness from the world. Instead, consciousness is always consciousness of something: It can't be cleansed of what it intends. Notable among Husserl's followers and critics are Merleau-Ponty (1964/1968) and Levinas (1961/1969) who inform the following arguments regarding the findings of this project. Their arguments problematize modern ontological presumptions, suggesting that the modern world as we know it is itself contingent, including the presumptions of an obtainable monolithic truth and the Cartesian subject-object dualism.

This and other related dualisms had been problematic for scholars involved in ontological speculation following Descartes. Descartes contributes to us the understanding that the individual plays a role in perception, that the world is not simply a given; our perceptions of the world don't directly correspond with the phenomena we encounter. Although doubts regarding the presumptions of natural understanding were philosophically and scientifically valuable, Descartes's conclusions generated new questions. The knowledge that perceptions of any individual are influenced by individual interests, saliencies, presumptions, sensory limitations, and so on, made problematic our understanding of a person's ability, while trapped within him/herself, to objectively understand his/her world at all. Somehow the pineal gland just didn't cut it. After all, a person could not be both subjective and objective. Two notable contingencies construct our conception of self in nature: self and nature. The assumption of an objective perspective is believed by many to be a satisfactory way (the only way) of knowing nature: empirical scientists believe they can know the world by bracketing their subjectivities and by submitting their observations to the scrutiny of their peers to validate their claims. Existentialists who criticize this perspective as naïve assume a more subjective posture in relation to the world, believing that perceptions of the world are always contingent and relative. The latter argue that how one knows the world is always in light of his/her own unique experiences. Neither of these perspectives, however, actually conform to how people engage the world. The objective empirical scholar does not drive his/her car in complete amazement as the landscape changes. The mind anticipates and intends the road ahead. Likewise, the more solipsistic person must contend with the fact that the contingent world s/he constructs is shared with others, that others respond in similar ways to the world as s/he does, and that intersubjective agreement *does* occur.

In an attempt to reconcile the dualisms that plague much of modern thought, Merleau-Ponty (1964/1968) introduced the notion of the "chiasm." The chiasm dissolves the presumed distinction between subject and object. Essentially, he argues that the human mind and the world function in complementary relationships. Instead of subject and object existing independently, he argues that the visible and the invisible exist coextensively; both are intertwined constituting relationship to the world. People and their behaviors *presume* a world "out there." Our actions are always in relation to the world we inhabit. We exist in relation to the world prior to the reflective consciousness that results in subjective awareness. In such relationships we cannot be abstracted from the world, an argument contrary to that of subjectivists; we do not live in our own world—before we recede into our own world we are already in the world. Likewise, the world we come to know is known only through the instruments available to us, that is, our senses. We cannot know the "true" essence of the world via our senses. We may know enough to survive in the world, but we cannot argue that the qualities of the world that are present to our consciousness constitute the world "as it truly is." The sea is perceived as blue, but blue does not constitute the sea. Though knowledge of physics, for instance, has been undeniably successful at enabling us to manage and engineer our environment, it is also true that the scope of that knowledge is limited to human capacity to conceive of it.

This intertwining of the individual with the world is Merleau-Ponty's (1964/1968) "chiasm." One can only know the world as someone subject to being known. The relationship of self and world and self and *others* is interdependent. He explains that, "between my body looked at and my body looking, my body touched and my body touching, there is overlapping or encroachment, so that we may say that the things pass into us, as well as we into the things" (p. 123). Thus, there are no clear distinctions between ourselves and the world we occupy. This has ontological significance because it rejects the idea that the individual can ever be completely liberated from his/her world. Liberty, when it functions to isolate the self, is a modern contingency that runs contrary to the way our waring minds actually exist in the world. Insular self-sovereignty tends to manifest itself in the stubborn presumption characteristic of today's culture: that individuals can be completely separate from others. This is a general characteristic of late modernism termed "atomism." Atomism manifests itself in human behavior and in the environments we design for ourselves. For example, Mumford (1989) describes what he believes are the inevitable outcomes of urbanization and suburbanization:

> ... the suburbanite renounces the obligations of citizenship at both ends; and the farther he goes from the center the more dissociated he becomes. ... These fast moving particles are the fallout of the metropolitan explosion. They are no longer held together either by the urban magnet or the urban container: they are rather emblems of the "disappearing city." But this movement from the center carries no hope or promise of life at a higher level. (pp. 502–503)

The conservative philosophy of unfettered free market forces (laissez-faire) also operates under similar assumptions; each person's success or failure is entirely contingent upon his/her own performance. According to the premises of the free market, if a person fails, s/he must have chosen the wrong path. In theory, everyone else gains from that failure, while the person who fails simply lives alone with the outcome. Thus, phenomena such as poverty are blamed on individual behavior, absolving society of any responsibility. As central as atomistic attitudes are to our culture, Merleau-Ponty's (1964/1968) ontology reveals the shaky ground upon which they are premised. Each individual is intimately enmeshed in a social fabric that plays a fundamental role in constituting his/her own subjectivity.

Though we are enmeshed, we are separate and unique. Merleau-Ponty (1964/1968) explains that interaction with an object in our environment involves the unexamined presumption of the other's gaze upon the same object. Things are encountered as though they constitute questions in need of answers, making evident the imperative of interaction and discourse. Employing symbols or language to name objects produces both the saying and the said. The said is eternal; it is our perspective shared and made available to the scrutiny of others. The ego is challenged with the realization that there exist alternative perspectives that challenge or affirm its statements. Subjectivity issues forth from the awareness of the alternative gaze.

Integral to the awareness and development of the self is alterity. It is not the differences already rendered impotent in equality that is fundamental but a radical alterity that not only determines one's subjectivity but is essential in its constitution. Here we find implications significant for democracy. As a response to the ontological concerns expressed by Husserl (1954/1970) and other phenomenologists, Levinas (1961/1969) rejected the pursuit of a monolithic truth or ontological unity—a "One" as he termed it. Avoiding ontological presuppositions that ground or justify violence between individuals, Levinas pursued an understanding of ethics between people. His arguments can be integrated with those of Merleau-Ponty (1964/1968) at the level of language; he recognized encounters with and discourse among strangers as central to the development of the subjectivity. Levinas (1961/1969) writes, "Language . . . offers things which are mine to the Other. To speak is to make the world common, to create commonplaces. Language does not refer to the generality of concepts, but lays the foundations for a possession in common" (p. 76). Without face-to-face encounters, the meaning of self, who the self is, and what the self has to offer remains unrealized, while an attitude presuming similarity or indifference remains intact. Rights, responsibilities, and justice remain abstract and foreign to this attitude.

The following argument opposes the notion that ego is inherent in the person (the static and nascent ego), and instead posits that self, as that upon which we reflect, is what emerges as a result of encounters with others. Levinas (1961/1969) makes this case well. "My being is produced in producing itself before the other in discourse; it is what it reveals of itself to the others, but while participating in, attending, its revelation" (p. 253). In our present social milieu characterized by atomism and disengagement, it becomes much more difficult for one to know one's self. As is made evident by Habermas's (1962/1989) observations, to understand the ego and the self one must confront and engage others. This means far more than simply *displaying* self in public space; as Levinas puts it, "Speech refuses vision, because the speaker does not deliver images of himself only, but is personally present in his speech, absolutely exterior to every image he would leave" (Levinas, 1961/1969, p. 296). Wearing a suit or a spiked blue Mohawk may announce to the world that you are conservative or are not, but the self on display is only *known* through the back and forth of dialogue, only revealed in the saying. The self is constituted in response to the other, and the other is always prior to self. Levinas (1961/1969) observes the self existing only in proximity to others. This certainly upsets the notion of a nascent ego waiting to be freed. The engaged self bares the marks of a refusal to abide by its own imperative; Levinas asserts that individuals are obligated or responsible to the other who commands the self and its horizons to become more expansive.

Admittedly, my explanation of Levinas' arguments place too much emphasis on reciprocity. He would never argue that one should tend to the other because of the personal benefits derived. To more closely approximate his argument, Levinas maintains that my obligation to the other is always a priori. We, in a sense, recede into nature until the other calls us forth. The other refuses to be mistaken as any other inanimate or animate phenomena in our field of experience and we are made subject to the other. "In the proximity of the face, the subjection precedes the reasoned decision to assume the order that it bears" (Levinas, 1947/1987, p. 112). There exists a preunderstanding (prior to reason) called forth by the encounter with the other that commands us. This is far different than more modernistic or collectivistic conceptualizations of this relationship, or what Levinas terms "fusion." Martin Buber (1970) describes the interpersonal relationship as a collective unit that privileges the self by demanding reciprocity. Reciprocity presumes the other has something the self reasons is valuable. Levinas grants Buber first place in recognizing the ground, the theme of the other (Levinas, 2001) but rejects the modernistic presumption that demands value from the other and reciprocity. Do we respond as we do toward others because they have something for us (predictable and quantifiable)? Or because of the wonderment and alterity they manifest? Levinas leaves his readers with the sense that the modern individual turns the latter into the former.

The imperative of the face of the Other, according to Levinas, escapes Husserl's intentionality. Though as a matter of practice the people we engage are often thematized by us, Levinas' point is that the Other *shouldn't* be thematized—that we should beware the role intentionality plays in categorizing people. Because of his/her alterity, the Other should be treated as astounding and irreducible.

> According to my analysis, on the other hand, in relation to the face, it is asymmetry that is affirmed: at the outset I hardly care what the other is with respect to me, that is his own business; for me, he is above all the one for whom I am responsible. (Levinas, 1983)

Vested with irreducible uniqueness we should resist thematizing the other and cope with the "traumatism of astonishment" experienced when we engage the Other through discourse (Levinas, 1961/1969, p. 73). The cultural tendency to presuppose similarity between others and ourselves is also what limits the possibilities of the development of unique subjectivity. It is the alterity of the Other that expands our possibilities of response to the world. Beyond the family, it is the community with its language, culture, and history that contextualizes and defines possibilities of meaning for the self. Thus, it is in these conflicting face-to-face encounters—the subjective disruption induced by alterity or the process by which the gaze of the Other makes an Other of ourselves—that ego is called forth from a slumber and perspective develops. The Same-ness just described should not be confused with the publicly engaged individual; this individual is not "of the collective" but is a unique subjectivity possessing individual will and is primarily concerned with justice. S/he doesn't compromise self by adhering to convention; instead, the self inadvertently evolves as others are accommodated in public engagement. The community that is constituted by language, culture, and history is that in which we find ourselves. And it is only in this context of community and accommodation that the developing self or ego can possess meaning. Without community self is meaningless.

But the community, according to Levinas (1961/1969), is more than an aggregate of others, or a delight in difference. The aggregate is galvanized, in a sense, by a concern for justice. The plurality demands justice, an objective order of sorts that allows us to know who goes first. Levinas writes, "Justice consists in again making possible expression, in which in nonreciprocity the person presents himself as unique. Justice is a right to speak" (p. 298). Justice is possible only if the other is heard and considered in his alterity and uniqueness. Likewise, without interaction, in the solitudes we generate amidst all the modern buzz of our culture, actual justice predicated on the individual voices (time) of the other is an impossibility.

Fostering and encouraging encounters for the reasons outlined is not some post-modern move wherein egos reign supreme (this is an apt description of our culture right now). The value of Gebser's (1949/1985) notion of the integral mode of consciousness is that it does not throw the rational baby out with the perspectival bathwater. The modern notion of objectivity is valuable to the extent that it gives society grounds for justice. Levinas (1947/1987) explains, "Objectivity issues from justice and is founded on justice, and is thus exerted by the *for-the-other*, which, in the alterity of the face, commands the ego" (p. 106). Levinas's notion of objectivity, however, is handled with care. He does not use it to describe some external and permanent order. Instead, from a phenomenological standpoint, objectivity constitutes a tool enabling consciousness to fathom order among cacophony, a purpose of objectivity that has been sedimented. Levinas tempers our current understanding of objectivity again with his understanding that objectivity functions to foster justice and not its own perpetuation. Most unique about Levinas's ideas of community is that he emphasizes responsibility by placing justice before liberty while drawing a careful distinction between the imperatives of justice and the necessities of order.

Levinas's sense of justice is not what Mr. Andrade experienced in his trial. Mr. Andrade was not heard. What was unique about the circumstances surrounding his crime was irrelevant according to a law that, prior to the crime taking place, precisely defined both the degree of his crime and the severity of the punishment. Nevertheless, this is the type of order for which many clamor in U.S. society, a nation that currently has more than two million people incarcerated (Vallis, 2004)—more than any other country. Clearly, this is not what Levinas (1981/2002) had in mind:

> ... justice is not a legality regulating human masses, from which a technique of social equilibrium is drawn, harmonizing antagonistic forces. That would be a justification of the State delivered over to its own necessities. (p. 159)

The justice our culture is presently pursuing encourages distance, automation, and outcome. So long as tranquility is maintained, members of the society are indifferent advocates of its procedures. Levinas's challenge to our contemporary notion of justice is premised on responsibility for the Other, responsibility even for the Other's responsibility. A difficult justice, but necessarily uniquely addressed to the needs of the Other. Contemporaneousness is central to his conceptualization—I am subject to each person. At the institutional level, there are no distinctions between the others as each bears an equal demand. To be just, we are called to the requirement that the Others be encountered, engaged, heard, and considered in light of their interests. These interests must be known, and ours known to them for the facilitation of effective and response-able democracy.

In sum, this argument does not make prescriptions for society to entertain the selfish concerns of each individual who speaks. I'm guilty of ignoring plenty of people. When I sink into my mindless mode of walking I find all sorts of people to ignore; street people I encountered in northern cities have been replaced by Christian proselytizers in the South. Ironically, I celebrate people willing to do these sorts of things, putting themselves out in public, willing to engage strangers. Admittedly, however, I presume to know what they are going to say and that it is of little value. While I won't be caught arguing that we need to listen to more people on the street, I maintain that my mode of walking is quite similar to the operation of society on a much larger scale. We keep voices closest to us that are familiar, safe, and consistent with our own while attributing little value to the voice of others. What is troubling is that our value of another's perspective is determined according to its contiguity with our own. Comfort derived from this behavior is the result of predictability—the cradling sense that comes from knowing what to expect from others and the world. With respect to the functions of government, the same applies. It seems we much prefer predictability to the kind of social change necessary to defeat political avoidance. Fewer voices enter the fray because of the overwhelming cultural directive to maintain stability, foster predictability, and ensure reliability—"Please take the wheel while I take a nap." Those who *do* get involved and are consequently *heard*—those who shape the national agenda—are people who don't think like the spectrum's center. According to them, the pot *needs* stirring—they have a bone to pick. Putnam (2000) notes, "The more extreme views have gradually become more dominant in grassroots American civic life as more moderate voices have fallen silent" (p. 342). Control of the political agenda has been yielded to the spectrum's extremes by a mode of consciousness that perceives political detachment as meritorious. The horizons of those directing our ship of state are unlike those in the political "center." Wattenberg (1991) explains that many individuals running for office no longer need parties because they are independently wealthy; their wealth enables them to fund their own primary campaigns. Their agendas are capable of being built with little reference to the needs of partisans and the compromises of their parties. Although many still believe that politicians of this sort establish policies in the best interest of voters, it is unlikely that their proposals and bills have emerged inductively through direct voter contact. I don't advocate raising "poll-driven" politics above some notion of leadership based in principle, however, it behooves so-called principled leaders to check how consistent their principles are with the principles (and immediate material needs) of their constituents.

WHAT ARE WE TO DO?

The value of this project is derived from the process of bringing to light the contingent ways swing voters assign meaning to their political environment. The issues addressed here can't be properly remedied without better understanding their causes. If at the root of the problem lies a peculiar adaptation of awareness, changing behaviors without challenging the mode of approach to social and political imperatives is unlikely to solve anything. Putnam recommends exploring innovative ways of rehabilitating social capital. Although the goal is commendable and is related to the arguments discussed in this book, the attitudinal barriers are enormous. Society, both socially and physically, has been constructed to reflect the values of separation, distance, and individualism—values inadvertently perpetuated by society's design.

A quick look at our community habits and contemporary families reflects how deeply the ethos of individualism is made manifest. Our families (those with whom we are most intimate and trusting) are scattering. Very few families in the United States house people beyond the nuclear unit of the two parents and their offspring. According to the 2000 U.S. census 75% of all households have 3 or fewer people living in them. In 1900 however, the average household had more than 4.5 persons, and almost half of U.S. citizens lived in households with six or more people. Only 3% of the 164 million individuals 30 years or older are grandparents who live in the same household with their own grandchildren (Hobbs & Stoops, 2002). Burchell and Listokin (1995) point out that from the 1960s to the mid-90s "the share of elderly living alone has increased by 50 percent" (p. 583). Many of our older citizens live on their own until it is impractical; Burchell and Listokin (1995) explain that at age 75 most "Americans divest themselves of most property, [and] move from retirement dwellings to senior care homes" (p. 560). Only rarely are they returning to their childrens' homes. According to the 2000 U.S. Census, only .07% of households were multigenerational (Multigenerational households, 2000), possessing three or more generations within one household.

Our cities are arranged accordingly, wherein city space is divided and devoted to their unique purposes. Sennett (1977) terms this phenomenon "single function urban development" (p. 297). Arranged this way, different classes live in separate communities divided from one another by city features like train tracks, roads, and expressways. Business areas are also separated from the community; consequently our commutes are longer. One can go to work in the business district in the city or away from the city in an industrial park and later recreate in a public park. Relatively new to this arrangement process is the separation by age. The notion of separating senior citizens from working age people and their children would have been considered an injustice not too long ago. Jobs change location now more than they used to, and when they don't leave the country altogether, individuals are quite often willing to move away from one's home neighborhood and state. U.S. Census Bureau statistics indicate that 45% of citizens move every five years (Gross migration, 2000). As a result, the older are separated from the younger. Whereas nursing homes represent the last stop in the community from family home to the ultimate end, Del Webb and other developers have introduced a popular alternative: communities designed exclusively for the senior population. In their literature they explain, "Active Adult Communities from Del Webb, we understand that you've worked hard, played equally hard, and achieved many goals along the way. Now your time is your own" (Active adult, 2004). Quite obviously, owning your time manifests as the luxury of spending it all by yourself. It is worth noting that many of these communities are restricted to adults only.

Overcoming these deeply entrenched attitudes and the consequent behaviors is a task only achieved by a reappraisal by our dissociative culture. Unfortunately, accomplishing this object is not uncomplicated. Society has to come to terms with the unexamined attitudes that have contributed to disengagement in the first place. Specifically, these phenomena include our atomistic tendencies and our ontological presuppositions that allow us to reason ourselves apart from one another. Again, this is not an appeal for a new collective in which all are same. Instead, it is a way of engaging difference that anticipates and embraces it as the inherent quality that makes living interesting in the first place.

Participation, however, would require us to become familiar once again with formulating our own thoughts—thoughts we believe are valuable enough to share. How do we as a society address Habermas's (1962/1989) claim that citizens have become information consumers as opposed to thought producers? As a society, we subject ourselves to information rather than risk becoming originators of communication. That people watch television too much is a matter of judgment. For some, television is a necessary release. For others, it is a companion. In any event, what is undeniable is that people in the United States submit to visual and aural stimuli that generates a kind of common ground serving the status quo. People cannot walk (cell phones, headphones, and PDAs), drive (cell phones, stereos, and sun-visor or headrest DVD players), or sit (cell phones, television, music, and video games) without bringing along some form of rich mediated entertainment. While watching the *Today Show* some days ago, I noted the camera filming a person outside showing his portable television to the television camera that was broadcasting his image to his own television. He seemed delighted with the irony. Confused? Or is this familiar and symptomatic of the technological dead end of communal possibility? I've seen children play video games, with another television on, arguing over what song should be playing on the stereo while trading back and forth their Gameboy between turns. Soon they will learn what my family sadly took years to understand—a television in each room guarantees fewer arguments. With the volume of information and noise we introduce into our environments each day we are increasingly strangers to our own thoughts and the thoughts of others.

Effecting urban design and media consumption would certainly alter how we live our lives, but I doubt that it is likely to happen soon in a culture that values space and craves stimuli the way we do. Thus, what follows is the obligatory appeal to the reader to think, read, write, and talk more than s/he does. This means overcoming the types of attitudes that equate discussion or debate with contentiousness or aggression. For instance, the thought of politicians getting along should be *more* disconcerting than the idea of them fighting. Primarily, their job is to represent their constituents' interests, which often involves disagreement between people who do not understand or appreciate those interests. Our job as citizens is not much different. We need to formulate and voice our opinions. What must be overcome to accomplish this undoubtedly involves re-evaluating the notion that there is merit in staying quiet, insulated. The idea that the swing voter, this objective political observer, only enters the discussion regarding the presidential race at the last second, while casting a vote, should be more reprehensible than anything else.

Finally, the practice of characterizing politics and elections as something that happens *to* voters maintains the presumption that voters are passive bystanders or political referees. Academics who study politics as well as the press and political practitioners need to keep in mind the larger context to which their messages apply. It is not enough to examine an election as an isolated episode or to view voter responses strictly as responses to discrete stimuli. For example, a voter rarely votes because of one advertisement, and if s/he does, it is likely because the campaign parameters failed him/her. Looking at the 2000 presidential election, it is too simplistic to state that swing voters played an enormous role because of the nature of *that* election (Bush versus Gore). The voters are as static as the political milieu—which is to say not very static. How that election was perceived is the result of both the events and arguments of that campaign as well as the larger context in which the election occurred. Thus, it is necessary to acknowledge relevant history, concerns, and attitudes of the swing voters that helped shape that election—to study the voter. It is my sincere hope that this has been accomplished in this text.

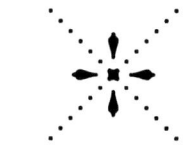

APPENDIX A

Transaction Writing Material

Subject # _____

Directions:
    1) Watch the following advertisement.
    2) Stop the advertisement when it is over.
    3) Answer the following three questions. Write as much as you want...take your time.
    4) You may rewind the video if you would like to watch it again. You may watch it as many times as you like.
    5) Once the first video is through, repeat these directions for the second video.

1. What do you think the advertisement means?
2. What is your reaction to the advertisement? How do you feel about it?
3. What are the most important parts of the advertisement?
4A) How did the advertisement make you feel about the candidate, George Bush?
4B) How did the advertisement make you feel about the candidate, Al Gore?

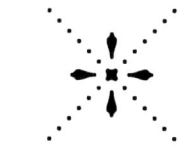

APPENDIX B

Advertisement Transcripts

BUSH SPOT: "NO CHANGES/NO REDUCTIONS"

Bush: We will strengthen social security and Medicare for the greatest generation and for generations to come.

Bush: I believe great decisions are made with care.

Image: Several seniors shown in succession against white backdrop. Fades into George W. Bush speaking.

Text: Governor George W. Bush

Image: Fade back to Governor George W. Bush speaking.

Text: Care

Bush: Made with conviction.

Bush: We will make prescription drugs available and affordable for every senior who needs them.

Bush: You earned your benefits. You made your plans. And President George W. Bush will keep the promise of social security, no changes, no reductions, no way.

Text: Conviction

Image: Senior woman getting blood pressure taken. Fades back to Governor George W. Bush speaking.

Text: Available prescription drugs.
Text: Affordable prescription drugs.

Image: Senior citizen playing softball.

Image: Seniors loading mobile home.

Text: Protect and strengthen social security.

Image: Fade back to Governor George W. Bush.

Text: Keep the promise.

Text: Bush/Cheney 2000

GORE SPOT: "COLLEGE"

Voice: Big corporations get a tax write-off for education or training for their high paid executives.

Voice: But for hard-working middle-class families you don't get enough help to afford your kids' college tuition.

Voice: Al Gore understands middle class families need help.

Image: Executive in board meeting.

Image: Executive making PowerPoint presentation.

Image: Mother helping daughter with computer.

Image: Two graduates in gowns walking outdoors with diplomas.

Image: Al Gore talking in a school assembly.
Image: Students smiling.

Image: Student studying in library.

APPENDIX A								157

Voice: $10,000 of college tuition tax deductible every year to help middle-class families send their kids to college.

Gore: We need help for middle class families to pay college tuition by making it tax deductible.

Gore: I'm for a life-long commitment to education.

Text: The Gore Plan: Make $10,000 of college tuition tax deductible.

Image: Two students talking in library.

Image: Students walking on campus.

Image: Gore kneeling with student at computer.

Image: Gore talking in school assembly with Liebermann.

Text: Al Gore for President

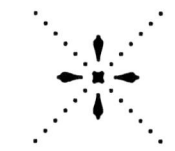

REFERENCES

Ackerman, K. D. (2003). *The dark horse: The surprise election and political murder of President James A. Garfield.* New York: Carroll and Graf Publishers.

Active adult communities by Del Webb. (2004). [On-line]. Retrieved February 16, 2004 from the Del Webb Corporation homepage: http://www.delwebb.com/activeadult/index.shtml

Ansolabehere, S., & Iyengar, S. (1996). Winning, but losing: How negative campaigns shrink electorate, manipulate news media. *The Quill, 5,* 19–22.

Austin, E. W., & Pinkleton, B. E. (1995). Positive and negative effects of political disaffection on the less experienced voter. *Journal of Broadcasting & Electronic Media, 39,* 215–235.

Bagdikian, B. H. (1997). *The media monopoly* (5th ed.). Boston: Beacon Press.

Barnouw, E. (1968). *The golden web: A history of broadcasting in the United States 1933–1953.* New York: Oxford University Press.

Berger, A. A. (2000). *Ads, fads, and consumer culture.* Lanham, MD: Rowman & Littlefield.

Bernstein, R. J. (1983). *Beyond objectivism and relativism: Science, hermeneutics, and praxis.* Philadelphia: University of Pennsylvania Press.

Breslau, K. (2000, August 28). Wooing wired workers. *Newsweek,* pp. 28-29.

Brooks, D. (2000). *Bobos in paradise.* New York: Simon and Schuster.

Buber, M. (1970). *I and thou.* New York: Charles Scribner's and Sons.

Burchell, R. W., & Listokin, D. (1995). Influences on United States housing policy. *Housing Policy Debate, 6*(3), 559-617.

Campbell, A., Converse, P. E., Miller, W. E., & Stokes, D. E. (1960). *The American voter: Unabridged edition.* Chicago: University of Chicago Press.

Campbell, J. E. (2000). *The American campaign: U.S. presidential campaigns and the national vote.* College Station: Texas A&M University Press.

Cantril, H., Gaudet, H., & Herzog, H. (1940). *Invasion from Mars: A study in the psychology of panic.* Princeton, NJ: Princeton University Press.

Caywood, C., & Preston, I. (1989). The continuing debate on political advertising: Toward a jeopardy theory of political advertising as regulated speech. *Journal of Public Policy, 8,* 204-226.

Colford, S., & Lafeyette, J. (1991, December 9). Political ads under fire. *Advertising Age,* p. 4.

Culler, J. (1984). *On deconstruction: Theory and criticism after structuralism.* Ithaca, NY: Cornell University Press.

Devlin, L. P. (1989). Contrasts in presidential campaign commercials of 1988. *American Behavioral Scientist, 32,* 389-414.

Devlin, L. P. (1993). Contrasts in presidential campaign commercials of 1992. *American Behavioral Scientist, 37,* 272-290.

Devlin, L. P. (1997). Contrasts in presidential campaign commercials of 1996. *American Behavioral Scientist, 40,* 1058-1084.

Devlin, L. P. (2001). Contrasts in presidential campaign commercials of 2000. *American Behavioral Scientist, 44,* 2338-2369.

Dewar, H., & Milbank, D. (2004, June 25). Cheney dismisses critic with obscenity; Clash with Leahy about Halliburton. *Washington Post,* p. A4.

Dowd, M. (2002, December, 5). The 1992 election disappointment—Road to defeat. *New York Times,* p. A1.

Downs, A. (1957). *An economic theory of democracy.* New York: Harper Collins.

Drumwright, M. (1993). Ethical issues in advertising and sales promotion. In J. Quelch (Ed.), *Ethics in marketing* (pp. 607-626). Homewood, IL: Irwin Publishing.

Faucheux, R. (2003, June). The 30-30 nation. *Campaigns and Elections,* p. 7.

Feder, R. (2001, October 26). Viewers aren't flocking to 10 p.m. newscasts. *Chicago Sun-Times,* p. 63.

Feder, R. (2002, June 6). '60 Minutes II' column gets readers ticked off. *Chicago Sun-Times,* p. 61.

Federal Elections Commission (2003). Voter registration and turnout in federal elections by age 1972-1996. [On-line]. Retrieved May 23, 2003 from http://www.fec.gov/pages/agedemog.htm

Fenwick, I., Wiseman, F., Becker, J., & Heiman, J. (1985). Dealing with indecision—should we . . . or not? In B. I. Newman & J. N. Sheth (Eds.), *Political marketing: Readings and annotated bibliography* (pp. 38-41). New York: American Marketing Association.

Ferguson, N. (2003, June 8). Why America outpaces Europe. *The New York Times*, Sec. 4, p. 3.
Fowles, J. (1992). *Why viewers watch: A reappraisal of television's effects*. Beverly Hills, CA: Sage.
Franklin, R. S. (2003). *Migration of the young, single, and college educated: 1995 to 2000*. U.S. Census Bureau. [On-line]. Retrieved April 20, 2004 from United States Census Bureau website: www.census.gov/prod/2003pubs/censr-12.pdf
Gadamer, H. G. (1977). *Philosophical hermeneutics* (D. E. Linge, Ed. & Trans.). Los Angeles: University of California Press.
Gadamer, H. G. (2000). *Truth and method* (J. Weinsheimer & D. G. Marshall, Trans.). New York: Continuum. (Original work published 1960)
Gearan, A. (2003, March 5). Supreme Court upholds California's three strikes law. [On-line]. *The Associated Press State & Local Wire*. Retrieved July 16, 2003 from Lexis/Nexus Academic Universe database: http://web.lexis-nexis.com/universe
Gebser, J. (1985). *The ever-present origin* (N. Barstad & A. Mickunas, Trans.). Athens: Ohio University Press. (Original work published 1949)
Geertz, C. (1973). *The interpretation of cultures*. New York: Basic Books.
Giedion, S. (1962). *The eternal present: The beginning of art*. New York: Pantheon Books.
Gitlin, T. (1983). *Inside prime time*. New York: Pantheon Books.
Goldstein, A., & Morin, R. (2002, October 20). Young voters' ennui skews politics: Graying electorate's issues predominant, fueling trend. *Washington Post*, p. A01.
Goffman, E. (1974). *Frame analysis: An essay on the organization of experience*. Evanston, IL: Harper Colophon Books.
Gross migration. (2000). *U.S. Census Bureau*. [On-line]. Retrieved February 8, 2004 from United States Census Bureau website: www.census.gov/population/cen2000/phc-t22/tab01.pdf
Gudykunst, W. B., & Kim, Y. Y. (1997). *Communicating with strangers: An approach to intercultural communication*. New York: McGraw-Hill.
Habermas, J. (1989). *The structural transformation of the public sphere: An inquiry into a category of bourgeois society* (T. Burger, Trans.). Cambridge, MA: The MIT Press. (Original work published 1962)
Hall, E. T. (1973). *The silent language*. Garden City, NY: Anchor Books.
Hart, R. P. (1999). *Seducing America: How television charms the modern voter*. Thousand Oaks, CA: Sage.
Henry, J. (1965). *Culture against man*. New York: Vintage Books.
Hesse, M. (1980). *Revolutions & reconstructions in the philosophy of science*. Bloomington: Indiana University Press.
Hobbs, F., & Stoops, N. (2003). *Demographic trends in the 20th century*: Washington, DC: U.S. Government Printing Office.
Hochschild, A. R. (1997). *The time bind: When work becomes home and home becomes work*. New York: Owl Books.

Holstein, J. A., & Gubrium, J. F. (1995). *The active interview*. Thousand Oaks, CA: Sage.

Husserl, E. (1960). *Cartesian meditations: An introduction to phenomenology* (D. Cairns, Trans.). The Hague: Martinus Hijhoff.

Husserl, E. (1970). *The crisis of European sciences and transcendental phenomenology* (D. Carr, Trans.). Evanston, IL: Northwestern Illinois University Press. (Original work published 1954)

Iyengar, S. (1990). Framing responsibility for political issues: The case of poverty. *Political Behavior, 12*(1), 19–40.

Iyengar, S., & Petrocik, J. R. (2000). "Basic rule" voting: Impact of campaigns on party- and approval-based voting. In J. A. Thurber, C. J. Nelson, & D. A. Dulio (Eds.), *Crowded airwaves: Campaign advertising in elections* (pp. 113–148). Washington, D.C.: Brookings Institution Press.

Jamieson, K. H. (2000). *Everything you think you know about politics . . . and why you're wrong*. New York: Basic Books.

Jensen, D. (2000). Data snooping, dredging and fishing: The dark side of data mining. *Special Interest Group on Knowledge, Discovery, and Data Mining: Explorations*, 52–54.

Johnson, A. (1978, September). In search of the affluent society. *Human Nature*, pp. 50–59.

Johnson, T. J., Hays, C., & Hays, S. (1998). *Engaging the public: How government and the media can reinvigorate American democracy*. Boulder, CO: Rowman & Littlefield.

Joslyn, R. (1984). *Mass media & elections*. Reading, MA: Addison-Wesley.

Kaid, L. L. (1981). Political advertising. In D. Nimmo & K. Sanders (Eds.), *Handbook of political communication* (pp. 249-271). Beverly Hills, CA: Sage.

Kaid, L. L. (1997). Effects of the television spots on images of Dole and Clinton. *American Behavioral Scientist, 40*, 1085–1094.

Kagay, M. R. (1991, August 22). After the coup; new heights for 2 Russians in U.S. poll. *The New York Times*, p. A18.

Katz, E., & Lazarsfeld, P. F. (1955). *Personal influence: The part played by people in the flow of mass communications*. New York: The Free Press.

Key, V. O. (1966). *The responsible electorate: Rationality in presidential voting*. Cambridge: Belknap Press of Harvard University Press.

Kirkpatrick, S. A. (1972). Political attitudes and behavior: Some consequences of attitudinal ordering. In D. D. Nimmo & C. M. Bonjean (Eds.), *Political attitudes & public opinion* (pp. 386–404). New York: David McKay.

Klapper, J. T. (1960). *The effects of mass communication*. New York: The Free Press.

Kohut, A. (2000). *Pew Research Center: Popular vote a tossup*. Washington, DC: The Pew Research Center.

Kramer, E. M. (1992). Gebser and culture. In E. M. Kramer (Ed.), *Consciousness and culture: An introduction to the thought of Jean Gebser* (pp. 1-53). Westport, CT: Greenwood Publishing Group.

Kramer, E. M., (1997). *Modern/postmodern: Off the beaten path of antimodernism.* Westport, CT: Praeger.

Lawrence, J. (2003, April 24). Gay rights issues scuttle GOP efforts at unity. *USA Today*, p. 8A.

Lazarsfeld, P. F., Berelson, B., & Gaudet, H. (1948). *The people's choice: How the voter makes up his mind in a presidential campaign.* New York: Duell, Sloan, and Pearce.

Leibniz, G. W. (1998). *Principles of nature and grace* (R. Franks & R. S. Woolhouse, Trans.). New York: Oxford University Press. (Original work published 1714)

Levinas, E. (2002). *Otherwise than being: Or beyond essence* (A. Lingis, Trans.). Pittsburgh, PA: Duquesne University Press. (Original work published 1981)

Levinas, E. (2001). Philosophy, justice, and love (1983). In J. Robbins (Ed.), *Is it righteous to be? Interviews with Emmanuel Levinas* (pp. 165-181). Palo Alto, CA: Stanford University Press.

Levinas, E. (1987). *Time and the others* (R. A. Cohan, Trans.). Pittsburgh, PA: Duquesne University Press. (Original work published 1947)

Levinas, E. (1969). *Totality and infinity* (A. Lingis, Trans.). Pittsburgh, PA: Duquesne University Press. (Original work published 1961)

Levine, R. (1997). *A geography of time: The temporal misadventures of a social psychologist.* New York: Basic Books.

Lucas, A.L., & Adams, W.C. (1978). Talking, television, and voter indecision. *Journal of Communication, 28,* 120-131.

Luther, M. (1990). *Three treatises.* Philadelphia: Fortress Press.

McLeod, J. M., Guo, Z., Daily, K., Steele, C. A., Huang, H., Horowitz, E., & Chen, H. (1996). *Journalism and Mass Communication Quarterly, 73*(2), 401-416.

Mead, M. (1953). National character. In A. L. Kroeber (Ed.), *Anthropology today.* Chicago: University of Chicago Press.

Merleau-Ponty, M. (1968). *The visible and the invisible* (A. Lingis, Trans.). Evanston, IL: Northwestern University Press. (Original work published 1964)

McGinniss, J. (1968). *The selling of the president.* New York: Trident Press.

Mills, M. (2001, March 21). Mind games. *Chicago Tribune*, pp. 5-1, 5-5.

Miroff, S., Seidleman, R., & Swanstrom, T. (1999). *Debating democracy: A reader in American politics* (2nd ed.). Boston: Houghton Mifflin.

Morgenstern, S. (1992). The epistemic autonomy of mass media audiences. *Critical Studies in Mass Communication, 9,* 293-310.

Morse, J. M. (1994). Designing funded qualitative research. In N. K. Denzin, & Y. S. Lincoln (Eds.), *Handbook of qualitative research* (pp. 220-235). Thousand Oaks, CA: Sage.

Morris, D. (1996). *The human zoo*. New York: McGraw-Hill.

Multigenerational households (2000). U.S. Census Bureau. Retrieved 2/7/04 from United States Census Bureau website: www.census.goc/population/cen2000/phc-t17.pdf

Mumford, L. (1934). *Technics and civilization*. New York: Harcourt, Brace, and Company.

Mumford, L. (1951). *The conduct of life*. New York: Harcourt, Brace, and Company.

Mumford, L. (1989). *The city in history*. New York: MJF Books.

Nadeau, J., & Barlow, J. (2003, July 15). Connoisseurs of the vacation. *Christian Science Monitor*, p. 9.

Nietzsche, F. (1974). *The gay science* (W. Kaufman, Trans.). New York: Vintage Books. (Original work published 1887)

Nimmo, D., & Sanders, K. (1981). *Handbook of political communication*. Beverly Hills, CA: Sage.

Noonan, P. (2003). *What I saw at the revolution: A political life in the Reagan era*. New York: Random House.

Ol' Dirty Bastard (O.D.B.) is once again a free man. (2003, July 29). *PR Newswire Association*. [On-line]. Retrieved May 23, 2004 from Lexis-Nexus Academic Universe database: http://web.lexis-nexis.com/universe

Ong, W. (1980). Literacy and orality in our times. *Journal of Communication*, 197-204.

Ong, W. (1982). *Orality and literacy: The technologizing of the word*. New York: Routledge.

Orlov, P. (2003, November 13). Betting on ODB? *Phoenix New Times*. [On-line]. Retrieved May 20, 2003 from Lexis-Nexus Academic Universe database: http://web.lexis-nexis.com/universe

Packard, V. (1957). *The hidden persuaders*. New York: Van Rees Press.

Packard, V. (1974). *A nation of strangers*. New York: Pocket Books.

Patterson, T. E. (1994). *Out of order*. New York: Vintage Books.

Patterson, T. E. (1998). *We the people: A concise introduction to American politics* (2nd ed.). New York: Overture Books.

Peirce, C. S. (1871). Fraser's the works of George Berkeley. *North American Review, 113*, 449-472.

Pelosi, A. (Producer). (2002). *Journeys with George*. Purple Monkey Productions.

Pfau, M., Diedrich, T., Larson, K., & Van Winkle, K. (1995). Influence of communication modalities on voters' perceptions of candidates during presidential primary campaigns. *Journal of Communication, 45*, 122–131.

Pocock, J. G. A. (1995). The ideal of citizenship since classical times. In R. Beiner (Ed.), *Theorizing citizenship* (pp. 29–52). Albany: State University of New York Press.

Pollock, J. (2003, February). The ten commandments of campaigning. *Campaigns and Elections*, p. 10.

Popkin, S. L. (1991). *The reasoning voter: Communication and persuasion in presidential campaigns.* Chicago: University of Chicago Press.

Portrait of America. (2001). *Issues: Before and after.* [On-line]. Retrieved February 16, 2001 from http://portraitofamerica.com/print.cfm?id-1526

Postman, N. (1986). *Amusing ourselves to death: Public discourse in the age of show business.* New York: Penguin.

Postman, N. (1990). *Informing ourselves to death.* [On-line]. Retrieved September 16, 2002 from http://world.std.com/~jimf/informing.html

Putnam, R. D. (2000). *Bowling alone: The collapse and revival of American community.* New York: Simon and Schuster.

Richey, W. (2002, Sept. 30). Bans on ex-con voting reviewed. *The Christian Science Monitor,* pp. 2-3.

Richards, J., & Caywood, C. (1991). Symbolic speech in political advertising: Encroaching legal barriers. In F. Biocca (Ed.), *Television and political advertising* (Vol. 2, pp. 231-256). Hillsdale, NJ: Erlbaum.

Rosenblatt, L. M. (1978). *The reader, the text, the poem: The transactional theory of the literary work.* Carbondale: Southern Illinois University Press.

Rousseau, J. J. (1978). *The social contract* (R. W. Crosby, Trans.). Brunswick, Ohio. (Original work published 1762)

Roszak, T. (1969). *The making of a counter culture.* New York: Anchor Books.

Sabato, L. J. (1981). *The rise of political consultants: New ways of winning elections.* New York: Basic Books.

Sabato, L. J. (1988). *The party's just begun: Shaping political parties for America's future.* Glenview, IL: Scott, Foresman and Company.

Schattschneider, E. E. (1975). *The semisovereign people: A realist's view of democracy in America.* New York: Harcourt Brace Jovanovich College Publishers.

Schor, J. (1991). *The overworked American: The unexpected decline of leisure.* New York: Basic Books.

Schudson, M. (1986). *Advertising, the uneasy persuasion: Its dubious impact on American society.* New York: Basic Books.

Schudson, M. (1994, Fall). Voting rites; why we need a new concept of citizenship. *The American Prospect,* pp. 59-67.

Schudson, M. (1998). *The good citizen: A history of American civic life.* Cambridge, MA: Harvard University Press.

Schudson, M. (2000). America's ignorant voters. *The Wilson Quarterly,* 24(2), 12-22.

Schuessler, A. A. (2000). *The logic of expressive choice.* Princeton, NJ: Princeton University Press.

Shannon, C., & Weaver, W. (1949). *The mathematical theory of communication.* Urbana: University of Illinois Press.

Schwartz, T. (1973). *The responsive chord.* Garden City, NY: Anchor Press/Doubleday.

Sennett, R. (1977). *The fall of public man.* New York: Knopf.

Showtime in the East Room. (2003, March 11). *Scripps Howard News Service*. [On-line]. Retrieved July 17, 2003 from Lexis-Nexus Academic Universe database: http://web.lexis-nexis.com/universe

Stern, B. B. (1994). A revised communication model for advertising: Multiple dimensions of the source, the message, and the recipient. *Journal of Advertising, 23*(2), 5-15.

Stewart, D., & Mickunas, A. (1990). *Exploring phenomenology: A guide to the field and its literature*. Athens: Ohio University Press.

Tierney, J. (2004, April 20). Using MRIs to see politics on the brain. *New York Times*, p. A1.

Time away from work gives Americans a kick in the career; Expedia.com survey reveals too many Americans put quality time on standby. (2003, May 21). [On-line]. *PR Newswire Association, Inc*. Retrieved July 21, 2003 from Lexis-Nexus Academic Universe database: http://web.lexis-nexis.com/universe

Tinkham, S., & Weaver-Lariscy, R. (1994). Ethical judgments of political television commercials as predictors of attitude toward the ad. *Journal of advertising, 23*, 43-57.

Tocqueville, A. de (1994). *Democracy in America*. New York: Knopf.

Tonor, R. (1992, November 4). The 1992 elections: President—the overview; Clinton captures presidency with huge electoral margin; wins a democratic congress. *The New York Times*, p. A1.

Triandis, H. C. (1995). *Individualism-collectivism*. Boulder, CO: Westview.

U.S. Census Bureau. (2001). *Median household income in 1989, United States by country 1990 decennial census*. [On-line]. Retrieved October 12, 2001 from http://factfinder.census.gov/servlet/StaticMapFramesetServ1et?_lang=en&_tm_name=DEC_1990_STF3_M0023&_SLSelected=010&_tab_gsl=50&geo_id=01000US&_caller=main

Vallis, M. (2004, May 29). U.S. beats Russia—at jailing: Leads in imprisonment. *National Post* (Canada), p. A13.

Van Maanen, J. (1988). *Tales of the field: On writing ethnography*. Chicago: University of Chicago Press.

Wattenberg, M. P. (1991). *The rise of candidate-centered politics: Presidential elections of the 1980's*. Cambridge: Harvard University Press.

West, D. M. (1993). *Air wars: Television advertising in election campaigns, 1952-1992*. Washington, DC: Congressional Quarterly.

Zaller, J. R. (1998). *The nature and origins of mass opinion*. New York: Cambridge University Press.

AUTHOR INDEX

A

Ackerman, K.D., 99, *159*
Adams, A.L., 10, 14, *163*
Ansolabehere, S., 13, *159*
Austin, E.W., 36, *159*

B

Bagdikian, B.H., 24, *159*
Barlow, J., 132, *164*
Barnouw, E., 15, *159*
Becker, J., 13, *160*
Berelson, B., 9, 10, 13, 14, *163*
Berger, A.A., 10, 25, *159*
Bernstein, R.J., 29, 34, 48, 49, 51, *159*
Breslau, K., 17, *159*
Brooks, D., 15, 98, *159*
Buber, M., 147, *160*
Burchell, R.W., 150, *160*

C

Campbell, A., 10, 14, 21, 24, *160*
Campbell, J.E., 16, 59, *160*
Cantril, H., 20-21, *160*
Caywood, C., 17, *160*, *165*
Chen, H., 36, *163*
Colford, S., 17, *160*
Converse, P.E., 10, 14, 21, 24, *160*
Culler, J., 31, 32, *160*

D

Daily, K., 36, *163*
Devlin, L.P., 8, *160*
Dewar, H., 113, *160*
Diedrich, T., 20, 24, *164*
Dowd, M., 117, *160*
Downs, A., 2, 10, 11, 26, *160*
Drumwright, M., 17, *160*

F

Faucheux, R., 15, *160*
Feder, R., 128, *160*
Federal Elections Commission, 36, *160*

Fenwick, I., 13, *160*
Ferguson, N., 132, *161*
Fowles, J., 138, *161*
Franklin, R.S., 142, *161*

G

Gadamer, H.G., 1, 18, 19, 31, 32, 33, 46, 48, *161*
Gaudet, H., 9, 10, 13, 14, 20-21, *160*, *163*
Gearan, A., 105, *161*
Gebser, J., 5, 11, 27, 48, 96, 97, 100, 101, 104, 106, 138, 148, *161*
Geertz, C., 18, 30, 39, 45, 49, 54, *161*
Giedion, S., 104, *161*
Gitlin, T., 16, *161*
Goffman, E., 23, *161*
Goldstein, A., 17, *161*
Gubrium, J.F., 45, *162*
Gudykunst, W.B., 31, *161*
Guo, Z., 36, *163*

H

Habermas, J., 98, 99, 118, 120, 121, 122, 123, 125, 126, 127, 128, 140, 146, 151, *161*
Hall, E.T., 23, 96, 137, *161*
Hart, R.P., 17, 25, 54, 64, 84, 130, *161*
Hays, C., 17, *162*
Hays, S., 17, *162*
Heiman, J., 13, *160*
Henry, J., 5, 121, 130, *161*
Herzog, H., 20-21, *160*
Hesse, M., 34, *161*
Hobbs, F., 150, *161*
Hochschild, A.R., 133, *161*
Holstein, J.A., 45, *162*
Horowitz, E., 36, *163*
Huang, H., 36, *163*
Husserl, E., 19, 47, 143, 146, *162*

I

Iyengar, S., 11, 13, 128, 129, *159*, *162*

J

Jamieson, K.H., 14, *162*
Jensen, D., 36, *162*
Johnson, A., 26, *162*
Johnson, T.J., 17, *162*
Joslyn, R., 13, 15, *162*

K

Kagay, M.R., 36, *162*
Kaid, L.L., 34, 35, *162*
Katz, E., 21, *162*
Key, V.O., 2, 9, 11, 12, 23, *162*
Kim, Y.Y., 31, *161*
Kirkpatrick, S.A., 13, 14, *162*
Klapper, J.T., 21, *162*
Kohut, A., 40, *162*
Kramer, E.M., 11, 33, 52, 95, 96, 101, 108, 142, *163*, *162*

L

Lafayette, J., 17, *160*
Larson, K., 20, 24, *160*
Lawrence, J., 15, *163*
Lazarsfeld, P.F., 9, 1, 13, 14, 21, *162*, *163*
Leibniz, G.W., 108, *163*
Levinas, E., 143, 146, 147, 148, *163*
Levine, R., 132, *163*
Listokin, D., 150, *160*
Lucas, A.L., 10, 14, *163*
Luther, M., 103, *163*

M

McGinniss, J., 22, *163*
McLeod, J.M., 36, *163*
Mead, M., 39, *163*
Merleau-Ponty, M., 143, 144, 145, 146, *163*
Mickunas, A., 19, *166*
Milbank, D., 113, *160*
Miller, W.E., 10, 14, 21, 24, *160*
Mills, M., 24, *163*
Miroff, S., 17, *163*
Morgenstern, S., 20, *163*
Morin, R., 17, *161*

Morris, D., 138, *163*
Morse, J.M., 40, *163*
Mumford, L., 5, 99, 102, 103, 107, 112, 122, 137, 145, *164*

N

Nadeau, J., 132, *164*
Nietzsche, F., 105, *164*
Nimmo, D., 20, *164*
Noonan, P., 116, *164*

O

Ong, W., 102, *164*
Orlov, P., 116, *164*

P

Packard, V., 5, 10, 16, 17, 22, 121, *164*
Patterson, T.E, 16, 110, 111, *164*
Peirce, C.S., 105, *164*
Pelosi, A., 114, *164*
Petrocik, J.R, 11, 13, *163*
Pfau, M., 20, 24, *164*
Pinkleton, B.E., 36, *159*
Pocock, J.G.A., 118, 119, *164*
Pollock, J., 8, *164*
Popkin, S.L., 2, 10, 11, 26, *164*
Portrait of America, 44, *165*
Postman, N., 126, 129, 130, 131, *165*
Preston, I., 17, *160*
Putnam, R.D., 5, 10, 20, 53, 121, 124, 127, 131(n3), 136, 149, *165*

R

Richards, J., 17, *165*
Richey, W., 118, *165*
Rosenblatt, L.M., 38, 43, *165*
Roszak, T., 93, 104(n5), 125,, *165*
Rousseau, J.J., 104, *165*

S

Sabato, L.J., 22, 94, *165*
Sanders, K., 20, *164*

Schattschneider, E.E., 17, *165*
Schor, J., 25, 132, 133, *165*
Schudson, M., 21, 109, 110, 111, 122, 131, *165*
Schuessler, A.A., 24, *165*
Schwartz, T., 16, 22, 23, 24, *165*
Seidleman, R., 17, *163*
Sennett, R., 99, 115, 121, 122, 123, 125, 141, 142, 150, *165*
Shannon, C., 21, 37, *165*
Steele, C. A., 36, *163*
Stern, B.B., 20, *166*
Stewart, D., 19, *166*
Stoops, N., 150, *161*
Stokes, D.E., 10, 14, 21, 24, *160*
Swanstrom, T., 17, *163*

T

Tierney, J., 17, *166*
Tinkham, S., 17, *166*
Tocqueville, A., de, 135, *166*
Tonor, R., 36, *166*
Triandis, H.C., 99, *166*

U

U.S. Census Bureau, 42, *166*

V

Vallis, M., 148, *166*
Van Maanen, J., 39, *166*
Van Winkle, K., 20, 24, *164*

W

Wattenberg, M.P., 2, 8, 9, 10, 11, 12, 13(n1), 16, 36, 72, 117, 149, *166*
Weaver, W., 21, 37, *165*
Weaver-Lariscy, R., 17, *166*
West, D.M., 16, 23, *166*
Wiseman, F., 13, *160*

Z

Zaller, J.R., 10, *166*

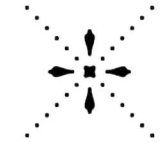

SUBJECT INDEX

A

absolutism, 105, 106
Affleck, Ben, 129
Alexander, Lamar, 116
alterity, 5, 135-152
 Other, 143
American dream, 138, 139
Andrade, Leandro, 148
anomie, 131, 142
Arthur, Chester Allen, 109
atomism, 27, 99, 124, 145, 146, 151
audimeters, 34
Australian-ballot, 110

B

Barr, Roseanne, 124
Begala, Paul, 127
Blair, Tony, 99
Bush, George H. W., 99, 116, 117
Bush, George W., 114, 115, 116
Bush, Jeb, 114

C

campaign practitioners, 7, 8, 20, 79
Carlson, Tucker, 127
Cartesian dualism, 38, 47-48, 143
Carville, James
Cheney, Dick, 113,
chiasm, 144
childhood, 123
civil disobedience, 99 , 123
Clinton, Bill, 78, 116
community, 27, 68
conspicuous consumption, 138
conventions, see public sphere
culture defined, 30-31
Cuomo, Mario, 114
cynicism, 78, 83-84, 90

D

Declaration of Independence, 123
Descartes, 51, 52, 143

decision making, 12, 25, 52, 70
  ground, 63, 80, 95, 131
  heuristics, 10, 11, 26, 52, 65, 80
  information, 25-26, 27, 63, 69, 79, 83, 87, 90, 100, 125-126, 129-130
  issues, 63
  low-information reasoning, 26
  party affiliation, 58, 72
  rationality, 11, 26, 111
  rational judgments, 22, 110
  reasoning, 63
  time constraints, 25-26, 27
deliberation, 120-121, 126-127
diaphaneity, 48
Dimensional Accrual/Dissociation theory, 11-12, 95-100
  archaic waring, 97
  dissociation, 136
  integral waring, 5, 48, 97, 143, 148
  magic waring, 5, 97, 107, 136, 138
  mental waring, 97, 138
  modern waring, 101
  mythic waring, 5, 97, 100, 102, 107, 136-138
  perspectival, 97, 104
  perspectival law of equivalences, 108
  waring, 97, 104, 107, 130, 138, 145
disenchantment with voting, 55
  nonvoters, 64
Dixie Chicks, 56
Dole, Elizabeth, 116

E

empiricism, 52
episodic framing, *see* mass communication
ethnography, *see* method

F

Florida recount, 57

Fox News, 127

G

Garfield, James, 99, 109
Gingrich, Newt, 78
Gore, Al, 115, 124, 127
Gore, Tipper, 115

H

Hannity and Colmes, 127
Hayes, Rutherford B., 109
hermeneutics, *see* method
horizons, 21, 32, 33, 46, 47, 48
horizontal society, 99
humanism, 124
Hume, 52

I

independents, 9, 11, 12, 61, 66
individualism, 4, 5, 99, 117, 131, 141, 143, 150
intentionality, 147

J

Jim Crow laws, 110
Johnson, Lyndon, 117
justice, 148-149

K

keeping it real, *see* private sphere
Kellogg plant, 132
Kerry, John, 124

L

late-deciders, *see* swing voters
Lazzio, Rick, 78
lebenswelt, 19
Lettermen, David, 117
lesser of two evils, 63-64
liberty, 5, 123-124, 141, 143, 145, 148
life-world, 19, 20, 142
Logan, Lara, 128
logical empiricism, 34
Lopez, Jennifer, 117, 129

M

Madonna, 124

Marin, Carol, 128
mass communication, 20
  effects research, 22-23
  framing theory, 128
  limited-effects paradigm, 21
  Magic-bullet paradigm, 21
McGovern-Fraser Commission, 110
meaning making
  audience role, 20
  context, 23
  oppositional reading, 32
  post-structuralism, 32
  reading, 31, 33, 46
  reader's response, 38
  structuralism, 31, 32
  political withdrawal, 79
media environment, 63
method
  active interviewing, 45
  analysis, 45-47
  critique of quantitative methods, 33-37
  ethnography, 18, 30, 36, 37, 38, 39, 40, 41, 49
  ethnographic interviews, 44-45
  hermeneutics, 18, 20, 24, 30, 31, 32, 33, 37, 38, 46, 53, 96
  hermeneutic circle, 47
  human science paradigm, 34
  informants, 39-43
  interviewing, 3, 42
  method of study, 37-49
  natural science paradigm, 34, 38
  phenomenology, 19, 32, 47, 53, 96, 143
  profile of informants, 42
  qualitative, 30
  recruitment, 41
  sampling, 40
  social science, 37, 39
metrics, 34, 36
modernity, 5, 51, 60, 97, 99, 104, 105, 143

modern swing voting ethic, 53, 93, 95, 100, 108, 135, 137
Mugwumps, 109, 110

N

National Election Studies, 12
natural attitude, 19, 47
Novak, James, 127

O

Old Dirty Bastard, 116

P

partisan disaffection, 11, 58, 94-95
partisan preference, 62
patronage, 110
performance based voting, 13
Perot, Ross, 66, 115, 116, 124
Pendleton Act, 109
penny press, 128
phenomenology, see method
political advertising, 1, 17
political attitudes, 29
political communication, 37, 125-131
political parties
  importance, 16
  weakening of appeal, 16
post-modernity, 5, 47, 48
private sphere, 95, 98, 99, 112, 113-133, 141-142
  keeping it real, 114, 141
Progressives, 109
Protestant work ethic, 131
public, 27
public sphere, 84, 95, 98, 99, 112, 113-133, 136, 141-142
  conventions, 100, 117, 122, 141
  courtesy, 123, 141
  etiquette, 122
  letters, 140
  origins of, 118

R

rationality, 5, 25, 51
Reform Party, 66

Renaissance, 51, 137
Rock the Vote, 56
Ryan, George, 99

S

Schwarzenegger, Arnold, 99
scientific voting, see swing voters
social capital, 150
social-desirability bias, 3, 60
Springer, Jerry, 128
subjectivity, 52
suffrage, 52, 109
swing voters
    abstainers, 17
    characteristics, 10-14, 135
    conscientious, 2
    defined, 7, 8, 18
    disengaged, 10
    extra-partisan, 2-3
    fairness, 75, 79, 90
    floating voters, 8
    late-deciders, 12, 13, 14, 59, 89
    lazy, 2
    leaners, 9
    limitation of voting models, 3-4
    middle voters, 15
    objective voters, 2-3, 52, 79, 90, see also modern swing voting ethic
    observations about
    operationalized, 30
    partisan, 3
    past research, 2
    scientific voting, 90-91, 111, 139
    September-to-November voters, 13
    switchers, 11
    ticketsplitters, 13

T

Talkback Live, 127
teleology of progress, 137
technocracy, 125
thematic framing, see mass communication
thick description, 45
time, 105-108
    decline in leisure, 133
    eternity, 106-107
    magic time, 106
    modern time, 105
    money, 137
    poverty, 131-133
    timelessness, 108

U

undecided voters, 8, 13, 14

V

validity, 34, 35, 37, 41, 46, 47-49
voting
    group think, 59
    objective voting, 4, 75
    voice, 59
    voters as jury members, 136
Ventura, Jesse, 115, 124

W

Wilson, Carnie, 129
Winfrey, Oprah, 115, 117

Printed in the United States
42002LVS00002B/49-114